BLACKNESS IS A GIFT I CAN GIVE HER

Blackness
IS A GIFT
I CAN GIVE HER

On Race, Community, and Black Women in Hockey

R. RENEE HESS

McCLELLAND & STEWART

McClelland & Stewart and colophon are registered trademarks of Penguin Random House Canada Limited.

Library and Archives Canada Cataloguing in Publication data is available upon request.
ISBN: 978-0-7710-0462-9
ebook ISBN: 978-0-7710-0463-6

Brooke Bergan, 'Argument 1' from *Storyville: A Hidden Mirror*, reproduced with permission from the author. Herbert H. Carnegie, 'The Future Aces Creed,' reproduced with permission from Bernice Carnegie.

Jacket design by Kate Sinclair
Jacket art: RichLegg / Getty Images
Typeset in Sabon by Terra Page
Printed in Canada

McClelland & Stewart,
a division of Penguin Random House Canada Limited,
a Penguin Random House Company
www.penguinrandomhouse.ca

1 2 3 4 5   28 27 26 25 24

Penguin
Random House
McCLELLAND & STEWART

*To Wendy Lillian Ramos (1979–2021) and to
my daughter, Lola. Everything I do is to make you proud.*

CONTENTS

INTRODUCTION

My Blackness is not objective. The world around me sees kinky hair, a high-yellow complexion with a fat ass, and attributes Blackness to me. Nothing I do, say, wear, like, or hate will change that—not my white mother or my 3/4ths white daughter. Proximity to whiteness will try and fail to define Black folks every single time. In a society built on the values of white supremacy and the social constructs of race, Black folks—and in my experience, particularly Black Americans—are forever destined to be categorized by the "one-drop rule," an identification created by white people to subjugate people of colour, specifically people of African descent. This is something that all Black people learn, although it took me years to truly comprehend it. It's something my mother and my daughter have yet to understand, but they are learning. The flip side of the social construct of Blackness is that the connection between Black folks—regardless of locale, background, or history—reverberates throughout Black communities. Our melanin binds us together, and for the purposes of this text, so does hockey.

Now, when I talk about Black women, I also understand that not all skinfolk are kinfolk. These sweeping statements are not meant to encompass everyone who identifies as a Black femme. We each have our own hopes, dreams, fears, and neuroses. While I work diligently to amplify Black voices and make room for representation, my act of storytelling is only a part of the narrative of Black folks. We are not a monolith. When I say "girls," understand I am talking about a spectrum of gender that includes anyone who might identify as a woman. By default, I advocate for Black women—including Black trans women—and this is a love letter to them.

I look back on my life at the Black women who have helped to shape me and get the distinct impression that they were trying to enrich my understanding of the world and of my own Blackness. Mrs. Smallwood, my eighth-grade English teacher, introduced me to Andrew Lloyd Webber's *The Phantom of the Opera*, the history of the Buffalo Soldiers, and a love of Black American literature. My mother's friend from work, Mandy, showed me my first batch of '80s Black horror films and sparked a lifelong obsession with the genre. My stepmother, Cathy, continues to show me the importance of forgiveness as she reveals the depths of Black love in the face of my father's fallibility. The passion and perseverance of Black women permeate everything I do. Black Girl Magic is a real thing.

When I first got into hockey, I understood that infiltrating the sport wouldn't be easy, but a few years after grad school, at an unsatisfying moment in my fledgling writing career, I wanted something new, something my own, something different. Hockey intrigued me, but at the same time, it felt completely unapproachable. *Everyone* knows hockey is a Very White

Sport! There are so few easily accessible entry points into hockey for Black folks, especially Black women. Hockey seemed like a mountain to climb, an arena that truly didn't want to be infiltrated by the likes of a Black queer woman like myself.

I've always loved a challenge.

My interest in hockey was initially sparked while attending an academic conference in Pittsburgh, Pennsylvania, in 2011. Three English honour society colleagues and I were in town for a literature conference, and ready to split our time between academia and sightseeing over the course of a week. I make a *mean* itinerary, but a hockey game, at the time, didn't even ping my radar. Still, in the City of Champions, I encountered hockey while eating tater tots and drinking Old Fashioned cocktails at Embury, a Prohibition-themed bar set up in an abandoned firehouse on the South Side that doesn't exist anymore. I noticed a hockey game on the television above the bar and asked about it. I don't remember what the bartender said exactly, but I recall him waxing eloquent about the 2009 Stanley Cup champions and letting me know that yinzers considered Pittsburgh a "hockey town." Later, driving back to our hotel, we got caught in the post-game traffic. Hundreds of fans were exiting the newly opened Consol Energy Center after a 1–0 shootout win against the New Jersey Devils, courtesy of James Neal—something I had no clue about at the time. Thinking back, that must have been a pretty intense game. I can imagine fans sitting on the edge of their seats, frustrated and tired, with no score for sixty minutes of play and then overtime in a game that went all the way to a shootout. I remember being annoyed at the traffic but fascinated by the fans celebrating in black and yellow on their way home, blocking the street, cheerful and slow.

Fast-forward a few years to when, in 2015, I came across an award-winning webcomic called *Check, Please!* circulating Tumblr. The artist and writer, a woman of colour named Ngozi Ukazu, told the story of Bitty, a figure-skater-turned-hockey-player at the fictional Samwell University. It was sweet and fun, and the game of hockey was central to its incredibly domestic narrative of teammates who spend a lot of time together. Questions about hockey, the game, and the fans came flooding back to me. This time I gave in to the nagging curiosity and decided to do a bit of research about the fourth most popular team sport in the United States. I took to YouTube and Twitter and found that the aesthetic of the game fascinated me. Hockey is fast. The players are skilled and athletic. The rules are simple and the game is exciting to watch. Still, I had no real idea of what my place could be in the hockey fandom. I just enjoyed the game. In fact, at first I knew of only two female friends who even watched hockey in real life, but they did so casually.

I've never casually joined a fandom in my life.

Much like Carl Hagelin on a breakaway, my love of hockey quickly gathered speed. I spent hours searching for statistics on players, exploring team media, and figuring out who I would cheer for. I decided on Western and Eastern conference favourites—the Dallas Stars and the Pittsburgh Penguins, respectively. Before financially investing in a sports hobby I wasn't sure would stick, I listened to game broadcasts and found that the Dallas colour commentator, Daryl "Razor" Reaugh, made me laugh with his "Razorisms" and clever turns of phrase. Mike Lange, the Penguins' radio play-by-play announcer at the time, also called the game beautifully, making me "smile like a butcher's dog" every time I tuned in to listen to him and Phil Bourque, known as the Ol' Two-Niner (in honour of his jersey number). Then, in 2016, the Penguins won the Stanley Cup and, just like that, I was all in. A team I had spent nine months loving, hating, cheering on, and generally developing emotions for had made it to the Stanley Cup Final and *won*. All of a sudden, the full experience of being a hockey fan opened up to me. I wanted to become part of the community, but I didn't know where to begin.

On a hot July day during the summer of 2016, the Stanley Cup came to Southern California and I had the chance to see the biggest trophy in sports at the Toyota Sports Performance Center in Los Angeles. Beau Bennett, who played with the Penguins until 2016, had brought the Cup to his old practice rink near his hometown, Gardena, having become the first-ever native Californian to win the Stanley Cup. My daughter and I drove two hours there and three hours back in traffic to take a picture with Beau and Lord Stanley's Mug. Earlier that same week, Beau had been traded to the New Jersey Devils. He only played in a single playoff game that year, but he still got a day with the Cup and brought it home to his fans. It was a magical moment that, in my mind, solidified my place in the hockey fandom, and helped me decide to enjoy this ride as far as it took me.

As I delved deeper into the world of ice hockey, I began to search for my niche. For a Black girl from California who didn't cheer for the home team, the task turned out to be more difficult than I'd initially thought. None of my local friends were into sports, so I was venturing into hockey alone. I started by scouring social media for open-minded, intelligent, and kind female fans, and engaged with mostly out-of-state white women on Hockey Twitter. We began to build a community while also centralizing our own interests and allowing room for learning and growth. Our group chat contained fans from all over, from England to North Carolina, and we had varied levels of knowledge about the game, but that didn't stop us from loving hockey and each other. These generally amazing, talented women with whom I cried and screamed and travelled to hockey games across state lines more accurately reflected my own values of inclusivity and allowed me to fall in love with the game of hockey in my own time. We talked butts and stats, messaged each other in our group chat during games, exchanged various media links, and even started a fantasy league. My "Sin Bin" sisters saw me through the growing pains of becoming a hockey fan, but as time wore on, a familiar refrain plagued me. *Where are all the Black folks in hockey?*

For Black folks, hockey seems like an entirely different world. The majority of players are white. The fans are white. The rinks are often located in white suburbs or, adversely, are located in marginalized communities while not effectively servicing the community within which the rink sits. The announcers and commentators are mostly white men. For a lot of Black folks, with large groups of white folks comes fear. Will that community accept a person of colour into their white space? What will happen to a Black woman when she infiltrates a space filled with white men? Is it safe? Is it worth it? From the outside, hockey seems like one of the more unwelcoming sports to people of colour. In the world of professional sports, hockey has largely remained culturally static in terms of fanbase and talent. There's little knowledge of Black folks' history in hockey, such as the Colored Hockey League of the Maritimes, Herb Carnegie, or Grant Fuhr, or the impact that Black people have had on hockey for more than 100 years.

When I truly started investing my time and resources into hockey, I quickly realized that the story of Black women in hockey had not been told. I went searching for books and films about Black folks in hockey, and the majority centred around Black men. The Angela James autobiography is the exception, as is Ms. James in most things. The Black men in hockey all know each other, they've worked together on projects, they've played together, they're friends. But what about Black women? Where do we fit in?

To find out, I headed to Twitter, a social medium I'd used somewhat successfully in the constraints of my previous work. In 2017, Black Girl Hockey Club began as a Twitter group chat with six or seven Black women hockey fans I had searched out on the app. The unique combination of Black culture and hockey culture invigorated us. A space where folks can find comfort in multiple identities feels good. We planned to get together and attend a live game. We wanted to take up space together. I soon realized that carving out a space for Black women within hockey—a notoriously cis, white, male sport—had the potential to become integral to our personal experiences with hockey, but I didn't initially understand the impact our unified voice might have on hockey culture as a whole. With the hope of meeting more Black women involved in hockey, I created social media accounts for Black Girl Hockey Club, or BGHC, and began to cultivate a network of Black women hockey players, fans, executives, and the folks who love us.

In 2018, I used BGHC Twitter to conduct a widespread research project that involved hockey fans of colour who interacted with hockey fandom in various ways. With a signal boost from journalists of colour like freelance writer Jashvina Shah and Charles Hallman of the *Minnesota Spokesman-Recorder*, as well as a few white co-conspirators in hockey media—namely Steve Dangle, who hosts the *Steve Dangle Podcast*, and Greg Wyshynski, who writes about hockey for ESPN—I was able to reach a wider audience of colour than I ever knew existed. After sending an innocuous tweet requesting POC to participate in a survey I'd created for research purposes, I received messages from men, women, and nonbinary folks from numerous different ethnic backgrounds, nationalities, sexualities, ages, and political affiliations who had one thing in common—the love of hockey. Through this survey, I found out that so many of them didn't feel comfortable going to hockey arenas, for various reasons that centred around the uncomfortableness of being categorized as "Other" in a very cis, white, male space. My goal became to share the joys of hockey with other Black women and marginalized fans who might appreciate the game of hockey but not enough to feel unsafe. It was obvious to me that we deserved a place in hockey that didn't yet exist.

The cold truth is, no matter how hard you cape for it, patriarchal whiteness won't save those of us who are not cisgender white men. The question is not "Will Black women gain equity within institutions built on systemic racism?" but rather "What can Black women build to subvert the systems of institutional inequity in order to create something better?"

When Black women create, we are able to manifest such joy, such inclusivity, that others who long for that same care become drawn to us and our work. Our Black Girl Magic benefits anyone who supports us and gives us the space to thrive. As I've said in a dozen interviews since 2018, "You don't have to be Black or a girl to be part of Black Girl Hockey Club"—although, if you keep reading, you'll find there are caveats to that invitation.

In the first year of its existence, Black Girl Hockey Club amassed thousands of followers and fans on social media. Professional teams like the Nashville Predators, New York Rangers, and Washington Capitals invited us to visit their arenas; sports media companies like ESPN and Sportsnet profiled the group, and the positive attention encouraged me to develop BGHC into a non-profit organization so that we could go to games together and give out scholarship money. BGHC started the 2019–20 season with the intention of creating something sustainable to benefit Black women. We planned a weekend of hockey and acts of community service with the Pittsburgh Penguins, and a HIFE (Hockey Is For Everyone) event with the New York Islanders. I travelled to North Carolina to tailgate with fans of the Carolina Hurricanes. BGHC began to gain steam and develop our programming. Then, COVID-19 hit. In March 2020, the same month that the world shut down to deal with the virus, Breonna Taylor was killed by police, who entered her home while she was sleeping and shot her during a no-knock raid of the wrong residence. And in May 2020, cordoned in our homes and terrified of the pandemic, the world watched as George Floyd was tortured for nine minutes and twenty-nine seconds—eventually murdered by a police officer named Derek Chauvin, surrounded by numerous witnesses, including other cops, by a knee to his neck.

Once again, Black folks organized, as we had for Sandra Bland, Philando Castile, Michael Brown, and countless others. With Trump in office saying the quiet part out loud and white supremacy becoming emboldened by anti-Black movements like Blue Lives Matter, tensions exploded onto the streets. Black women were leading organized and powerful protests in cities all across the United States and the world. What was a fan group like Black Girl Hockey Club meant to do in the face of blatant systemic racism? How could we authentically engage with and represent Black women in hockey during such tumultuous times? I began to question my own ability to lead BGHC in the midst of such a movement. How could I, a biracial Black woman who had only discovered hockey a few years ago, even begin to address the gatekeeping, the hiring discrepancies, the on-ice racism, and the off-ice collaborations with organizations and individuals who discriminate against marginalized groups? After such an exciting inaugural season, what would it look like if I—and BGHC—began to criticize the systems of a major professional sports league that had welcomed our group with open arms?

I worked to reconcile within myself that the league that had helped facilitate the growth of BGHC through media promos and in-arena interviews was the same hundred-year-old institution with little to no non-white, non-male leadership across clubs in both Canada and the United States; that there continued to be a culture of anti-Blackness cultivated in hockey that no professional organization had adequately addressed; that the only sports journalists even talking about race and hockey were racialized folks themselves. So, when the Black Lives Matter movement began to polarize communities during the Trump administration in the States, I wanted to acknowledge not only the racism in hockey directly, but also the ways I had devalued myself and other Black women. I started with an apology and a promise to do better. I had been holding myself up to the societal standards of colonizers, and I had been destined to fail. How could BGHC ever truly make a space for Black women in hockey without us first taking care of ourselves? How could I ask others to put Black women first when I myself had been more concerned with success in the world of hockey than how to safely exist in hockey? I had been told, "That's just how the game is played," and I, determined to gain a seat at *their* table, had used that to excuse my own desire to be accepted by whiteness.

When my personal priorities shifted, so did the direction of the organization I had founded. We couldn't leave our homes to do meet-ups, so instead, BGHC held digital hangouts. We hosted educational panels and celebrated Juneteenth together. We talked about self-care. We started the BGHC Bookclub. I took time off from talking to the press, and when I returned, I prioritized speaking with Black journalists and non-Black co-conspirators who were willing to push and be pushed. I said the names of our dead and brutalized siblings, both publicly and privately. I asked BIPOC supporters of BGHC to talk about their experiences with the media. Alongside many BIPOC peers working in sports, I spent the summer of 2020 connecting a collective of Black players, fans, parents, and executives with one another. Non-Black journalists and influencers were asked to step up and use their power to advocate for those of us not in the room where it happens. The Black Girl Hockey Club board of directors expanded and built new programming across multiple fields and platforms, while our volunteer pool continued to grow exponentially. In Black Girl Hockey Club, it is Black women who are in positions of power, who are listened to, who are developing ideas and creating space for others. It is our stories that are shared and that build meaningful discussions. I can't help but breathe a sigh of relief that I am part of a space filled with folks who look like me in, of all places, hockey.

As a student of anthropologist and author Zora Neale Hurston, a sometime writing teacher, and a full-time empath, I am fascinated by the cultural experiences Black folks share in hockey, especially Black women. In fact, the motivation to work for equity in hockey comes from these stories. As the business side of my newly formed non-profit organization began to level out and we all learned how to balance COVID-19 and capitalism, I went back to some of the early discussions I had with Black folks in hockey. I picked up that thread again, and spoke with players, fans, mothers, professors, writers, and executives who I had gotten to know through my work with Black Girl Hockey Club. Blake Bolden and I met before BGHC ever existed, and I looked back on an early 2018 interview with her, and scheduled another. And another. Saroya Tinker had joined the BGHC scholarship committee and started the Saroya Strong Mentorship Program. I wanted to know why the BGHC mission was so important to her—and to her parents, who had joined me at a Pittsburgh Penguins meet-up in February 2020. I spoke to Bryant McBride, who spearheaded what is now known as the NHL's Hockey Is For Everyone initiative in the 1990s, about early morning hockey practice with his mother. I met with Sarah Nurse, who, as of 2023, was still the only Black woman hockey player to have played in the Olympics.

In interview after interview, commonalities emerged. We want to tell our side of the story and be heard. We want to feel cared for in the sport that we love. We want community and resources and equitable hiring practices. There is a tremendous vulnerability in Black women that is not often explored in popular media. The stereotypes applied to Black women involve our strength and resilience. Our wellness, our dreams, and our desires come second to the needs of our kids, our partners, our communities. Where can we find comfort if not in each other? Who will prioritize our needs if not ourselves? In 2020, it felt as if the world was crumbling around us, so Black women in hockey banded together to build something that continues to grow and shift, and includes other marginalized folks and allies within the sport of hockey. We impart gentleness and care onto one another and that spills out onto those who surround us. We speak truth, and others find value and instruction in our words.

Don't get it twisted, though. This is our story.

Baby's First Hockey Game

My first-ever hockey game, I remember standing in line, waiting for the gates to open, and this little old white lady and her friend, probably both in their seventies, started talking to me. I told them that I was local, coming to see the Dallas Stars play the Anaheim Ducks as a last-minute decision on a Friday night, and I also had tickets to see them play four days later in Los Angeles, against the Kings. The one woman laughed and let me know that she and her friend had travelled from Colorado to California to follow the team on their entire West Coast road trip. Anaheim, San Jose, Los Angeles, and then back home to see the team play the Colorado Avalanche. Now that's how you do retirement! Granny then proceeded to ask me if I had seen the Tyler Seguin *Sports Illustrated* "Body Issue" photo shoot. *Yes ma'am!* The Zamboni, the toque, a red, white, and blue popsicle, and nothing else? I can visualize it now. Art, I say! And a fan favourite. I may have pulled up a JPEG of one of the magazine images that I had saved on my phone for just such an occasion. She loved it, and as we walked into the Honda Center, I had high hopes that this was going to be a good time.

Before BGHC, before I'd even stepped a toe into a hockey arena, I knew that as a Black girl, I was going to be the odd duck and that there wouldn't be a ton of melanin in the space. I was right, but I couldn't focus on that, there were my boys! I headed down to the tunnel area to watch the players come out for warm-ups, not sure what I was doing but *stupid* excited to do it. Between me and the glass stood a sea of white folks all there for the same reason as me—to have a good time and to see our team. I must have squealed too loud, or looked too excited, because I remember a kid—twentyish, cis-male presenting, white, basic AF—telling me to "calm down" and laughing at my joy with his friends, regulating how I engaged with the game of hockey and comfortable with lessening the happiness of a stranger. Not knowing anything about me, this young man was determined to gatekeep hockey from me, even though we were both at the glass, both with our cameras out, both trying to enjoy the moment.

That's what I think of when people ask me about my first hockey game, but I've never told anyone about it, mostly because my public-facing goal is to focus on Black joy and not Black trauma. I'm also embarrassed. Maybe I should have said something to this kid, who was about the same age as the students at the university I work at, and called him out for calling *me* out!? Sometimes I imagine what I would have said to him, or what I would say to him now that I am *Madam Black Girl*

Hockey Club, hockey bigwig, community leader, yada yada yada. I'm still not sure.

Considering most of the people outside of BGHC that I speak to about hockey are white, I honestly don't bring it up because the incident is a jarring image of the reality of hockey. Racism, misogyny, sexism, ableism, homophobia, and transphobia take place in hockey spaces all the time. It's easy to ignore discrimination when it's not happening to you, and it's easy to prioritize intention over impact. It isn't fun to realize that a space you love might not be welcoming or safe for everyone. In fact, some folks would rather not mix social issues with sports at all. But the reality is, athletes, fans, executives, and everyone in between have intersectional identities impacted by the society in which we live. *Continuing to do things the way they have always been done benefits the oppressor.* I encourage allies, use whatever power you've got to facilitate an equitable, more diverse, safer environment for all in the spaces that you occupy. And I encourage marginalized folks to organize.

While micro- and macroaggressions happen to me in hockey spaces, those moments do not define hockey for me. There is a picture of me at that Stars game, my first ever live hockey event—the first of two that week, and the start of something really beautiful and life-changing for me. In this picture, I'm grinning like a fool, in the stands, bright red lipstick and brand-new green Stars hoodie, right before some random dude tried to kill my vibe. When I think of that night, I think of how I felt when I took that picture. I was at the start of a new hobby, one that would take my skills, my values, my strengths, and my emotions to unparalleled heights. And I had no idea what I was getting myself into, because let me tell you, this sport can sometimes feel like straight-up trauma. I often wonder if I'm doing the right thing, the right way, and if I even have anything to offer this community. But then I think of the pure, unadulterated joy portrayed in that picture, and how much I actually love hockey and the people I've met because of this sport, and I figure this is as good a space as any to plant my roots and facilitate some positive change.

So, fuck that guy. I'm not going to let him or anyone else rob me of the joy that hockey brings me, and neither should you.

CREATING OUR OWN NARRATIVES

Archetypes have always fascinated me. In graduate school, the concept became a bouncing-off point in much of my writing, and it is something I continue to examine with students when I teach any sort of writing or literature course at the university level today. The notion of shared cultural definitions, a way of understanding the world through symbols, colours, shapes, imagery, language, story patterns, and settings, can actually be quite beautiful and comforting. Fairy tales and fiction have been following archetypal patterns for centuries. From Snow White, a "damsel in distress," to Captain America, a quintessential depiction of Joseph Campbell's "hero," archetypes persist throughout society and help us understand the shared world around us. There are archetypes specific to various cultures, including African literature, but throughout "classic" literature and right here in North America, our collective understanding of cultural archetypes has been laid out by cisgender white men with the power, privilege, and opportunity to disseminate information.

In order to understand the harm that archetypal definitions can do to marginalized folks, particularly Black women, readers must accept the premise that the institutions that create and promote these stereotypes benefit from negative depictions of disenfranchised communities. In literature, film, and social media, stereotypes based in racism and misogyny— such as the "angry black woman" or the "mammy"—place Black women in a box, removing the opportunity for growth or nuance. Zora Neale Hurston spent her career studying Black American culture and subverting harmful stereotypes of Black women with works such as *Their Eyes Were Watching God*, writing multifaceted Black women characters in her fiction and using her own anthropological studies to create a new narrative. Afrofuturist writer Tomi Adeyemi world-builds a YA narrative full of non-white main characters, led by a fierce, emotional, powerful, and inconsistent heroine, in the *Legacy of Orïsha* trilogy. Various characteristics such as "strong," "resilient," "sassy," or "angry" are imposed on Black women, but these lack depth, are ultimately rooted in colonialism, and regularly cause harm. Society doesn't give Black women the room to create our own narratives, and so it fails to give us the opportunity to be soft, sad, or even selfish without heavy repercussions.

In their 1977 published statement, the Combahee River Collective focused on "a combined anti-racist and anti-sexist position" unique to Black women, who occupy a marginalized space in terms of both race and gender. The collective was a group of Black feminists who had been meeting for three years before they released their statement to the world. All members participated in a variety of progressive movements, in which they sought to analyze and develop practice around what we now know as intersectional feminism. By putting down on paper the experiences of Black women and naming the unique positionality of the intersections that we hold, the collective created an opportunity for others to recognize and engage with the work of radical Black feminism. When Black women are given the space and the resources to gather data and disseminate information about our own experiences, we are able to reimagine potentials and create intentional and intersectional community spaces that benefit *all* marginalized folks.

In order to build a better community for hockey and truly make the sport for everyone, Black women must work outside of traditional organizational power structures—particularly in sports spaces owned and operated by non-Black people. By restructuring the power dynamic in sports to not only include Black women but also place us in positions of leadership and decision-making, sports organizations have the opportunity to spread the valuable lessons of intersectionality throughout their ranks. But that is just the beginning of reimagining what sports might look like when Black women are given power over our own experiences.

While there is more multicultural representation in hockey these days, it is important to note who is telling our stories. The lack of qualitative and quantitative information about Black women in sports is glaring, but nowhere more so than in ice hockey. Even anecdotally, youth leagues don't keep track of "racial" information; Title IX, a Department of Education mandate meant to protect people from discrimination based on sex, doesn't serve Black athletes in an equitable way; and academic research that focuses on the Black experience in sports is most likely written and published by white people. But while much of the hockey research that is currently published lacks the dimension of intersectionality, a discussion of race, community, and making space for Black women in hockey can be found in the work of academics like Dr. Sabrina Razack, who wrote her Ph.D. thesis on Black Girl Hockey Club and spent a number of weeks in 2021 interviewing me, our volunteers, board members, and colleagues for her project. Together, we looked at some of the most prevalent current-day stereotypes placed on Black women in various sports, and the problematic basis of those stereotypical depictions. We also examined the concept of "joy as a mode of resistance" within an organization such as BGHC, which is led by Black women and focuses on the inclusion of Black women in hockey.

Dr. Razack and I met through a mutual colleague, Dr. Courtney Szto, who is part of a thriving anti-racism network in hockey spaces—occupied by academics, media folk, fans, and players. Dr. Szto's "Policy Paper for Anti-Racism in Canadian Hockey" (2020) has become a seminal text in discussions of race and hockey, lauded publicly by Canadian scholars and sports media as a clear path toward equity and inclusion for non-white players. Describing herself as a Chinese Canadian "settler scholar," Dr. Szto is an assistant professor at the School of Kinesiology and Health Studies at Queen's University whose research focuses on the intersections that create social (in)justice as they pertain to sport and physical activity. Her first book, *Changing on the Fly: Hockey through the Voices of South Asian Canadians*, unpacks racialized experiences in hockey as a way to explore notions of citizenship and belonging.

In 2020, Dr. Szto began volunteering with Black Girl Hockey Club on the "Get Uncomfortable" advocacy campaign committee, and has helped create educational material and lead workshop discussions on the intersections of BGHC and the work she has devoted her life to. In 2021, she reached out to pitch me the research project that would become Dr. Razack's Ph.D. thesis. We spoke about the origins of BGHC on social media, how BGHC utilized Twitter, Instagram, and our newsletter to engage audiences, and the characteristics of these modes of communication that are unique to Black women.

Dr. Sabrina Razack is an Indo-Caribbean Canadian from Pickering, Ontario, and began following Black Girl Hockey Club on social media in 2019. She comes from an impressive lineage of Black women doctorates whom I was lucky enough to meet at her dissertation defence in June 2022. As Dr. Razack worked toward her terminal degree in Kinesiology and Physical Education at the University of Toronto, she watched BGHC evolve from a social media community campaign to an international hockey clearing house in the space of a year. Dr Razack and I run in similar circles, but while I had strayed from the academic side of sport to do grassroots organizing work, she was using her thesis to tie together the practical and the academic, drawing on BGHC as primary research to illustrate the sociopolitical impact of Black women in sports spaces. Dr. Razack and I hoped that our conversations would be mutually beneficial, as well as helping others in hockey spaces.

After discussing the project and getting approval from the BGHC board of directors, Dr. Razack began to schedule interviews with not only me but Black women hockey players Blake Bolden and Sarah Nurse, BGHC board members Fatou Bah and

Dr. Tunisha Singleton, and even some of our non-Black volunteers. It was interesting to watch the project take shape from the outside, with folks randomly letting me know that they had spoken about me and BGHC to Dr. Razack, and asking did I know her work? Observing the academic exploration of Black Girl Hockey Club and our connection to a larger Black feminist movement led by scholars such as Audre Lorde and bell hooks inspired me to chronicle the space that Black women take up in hockey in this very book, using my own experience with research and storytelling. To be part of the narrative while simultaneously trying to observe, record, and preserve the narrative feels very meta, honestly, and kind of weird.

Dr. Razack's research not only helped me understand the historical importance of my work in creating Black Girl Hockey Club, it also reiterated the cultural value of storytelling within Black communities, and the power that narrative control wields in civilized society. As we explored these distinctions in our respective fields of study, we started with archetypes. Initially, we wanted to shape a new definition for Black women, *by* Black women, to counteract the harm of the many stereotypes based on racism and misogyny that have been placed on us. However, we soon realized that in order to engage with sport using the intersectional framework of Black feminism, our goal must be to deconstruct the entire *idea* of Black women as archetypes. The Combahee River Collective statement reminds us that the liberation of Black women is not only necessary but valuable, because of our inherent humanity. We are not simply the stereotypes ascribed to us: mammy, slut, dyke. We are so much more. We are complex, creative, and cool. And who better to champion Black women than Black women ourselves?

Although Black culture is popular and even trendy, we must remain wary of representation replacing research, and visibility taking the place of true systemic change. As Dr. Razack puts it, "the illusion of representation . . . masks the matrix of systemic racism. You can hire as many people as you want in commercials, but if your systems and policies and your hiring practices haven't changed, I don't really care if there's a reporter that, you know, quote, unquote, looks like me." The nuances that come with the intersectional space Black women occupy actually make it quite harmful to delineate said group within any particular trope; Black women cannot be defined as individuals who check off certain boxes in order to appease white audiences, and nor should we be satisfied by representation as performative action.

In order to evaluate the impact of Black Girl Hockey Club and the women at its helm, we have to first recognize that the success of such endeavours has yet to be measured adequately in typical (read: white-male-led) academic research. Much of the current published research on social activism in sports spaces is conducted and written by white people who are exploring the ways in which intersectional identities (ones they don't share) affect the larger athletic community. It is the lack of representation in sports history, media, publishing, and academia—and in hockey, it is the lack of Black faces on the ice, behind the bench, and in the C-suites—that forces marginalized folks into giving ownership of our stories over to institutions that may not have our best interests in mind. Texts that examine the specific impact of intersectional identities of Black women in sports include *A Spectacular Leap* by Jennifer Lansbury, which expounds on the ways Black women represent their communities by participating in athletics and explores the individual stories of Black women sports stars and how they interact with race, class, gender, and social justice issues, and *Passing the Baton* by Cat M. Ariail, which reveals the impact Black women in track had in shaping American social structures throughout the twentieth century. Both books were written by white women.

It is obvious that the success, values, and needs of marginalized communities cannot be measured adequately due to a lack of representation in societal positions of power. Less obvious and more insidious is the fact that within many of our institutions, there is a distinct desire by those who are in power to avoid engaging in race-related study in any sort of meaningful way, as it might reveal the depth of privilege and racism in these institutions and lead to a shift in power structures. In his essay "White Ignorance," Dr. Charles W. Mills, a London-born Jamaican philosopher, examines the concept of wilful cognitive dissonance toward the racism inherent in white privilege. Dr. Mills passed away in 2021, but his work on epistemology, white supremacy, and structural racism established a number of theoretical cornerstones on race and culture in contemporary Western philosophy. In "White Ignorance," Dr. Mills writes that the gendered and racialized marginalizations within American culture are a *feature* of American politics, not a bug. He recognizes that the concept of an "egalitarian and inclusive" America systematically excludes anyone who is not a white male. The performance of white ignorance suggests that some white people work very hard to convince themselves that inequities are only a "deviation" from a true equality available to everyone, as opposed to being built into systems designed to oppress marginalized folks and uplift white supremacy.

Instead of examining laws and policies that contribute to oppression, more often than not institutions fail to implement the research, researchers neglect to develop the data, and therefore the data doesn't exist and the realities can be ignored. But academic activists like Dr. Sabrina Razack and Dr. Courtney Szto use intersectional tenets to engage in sports activism and theory as they work to tell our stories, while identifying with particular marginalized communities themselves.

Instead of attempting to define Black folks in hockey, we must look to leaders with diverse experiences and skill sets to create a unique and ever-changing narrative of our shared experiences—from sports scholars to sports media companies led by Black women. For the African diaspora, writing, story-telling, and narrative-spinning is liberation. Often, Black women are stereotyped, categorized incorrectly, placed in racist and misogynistic boxes, and our experiences are unceremoniously dismissed. Our contributions to culture, society, and politics must be recorded accurately, and Black folks should be given the space to lead the way. Anecdotal and qualitative data is vital to building an infrastructure of knowledge in all fields, but when the majority of current sociological and anthropological data is gathered, analyzed, and disseminated by white males, marginalized communities are harmed. When marginalized folks chronicle our own experiences and those of our ancestors, when we name false narratives and push against systems of oppression publicly and consistently—like Dr. Mills did with his work—we contribute to a legacy of qualitative information that benefits Black communities everywhere, even in ice hockey.

I ask Dr. Razack what she thinks bell hooks and Audre Lorde might say about us trying to understand the impact of Black women on hockey using categorizations developed by research systems and institutions steeped in white supremacy. She stills, her features becoming thoughtful as she frowns at me through the computer screen before answering.

"I don't think they'd be impressed, per se. I think that they would be more focused on the reconceptualization of power, and how within the patriarchal system, power equates to dominance and exploitation of others. The power of Black Girl Hockey Club and reconceptualizing how you all assert your power; publicly being able to display your grievances. How you conduct your organization, the consensus, and having it open. It's kind of like, even though you're at the helm, [BGHC] does appear to have this kind of horizontal leadership aspect to it with the different committees and how you kind of share that power within the group, at least that's my view of it. That's what I would want bell hooks to look at . . . that you are holding up the tenets of a Black feminist activist movement.

"These movements are being co-opted, sanitized. They're trendy. It's *still* trendy. I don't know. I want to say I have hope in white people some days and other days I . . . I don't know if I can say I have hope. There's always the commodification, or the attachment of Black culture . . . the lines are a bit blurred with activism and that too, right? I think right now, for people to be attached to this too, it's, you know, it's kind of a trendy thing . . . how people are attaching themselves to Black Girl Hockey Club and even you yourself. I think that there's also a bit of hesitancy from you and a bit of discomfort, rightfully so."

I often lament the media coverage, attention, and public focus on *me*, as opposed to the message of Black Girl Hockey Club. Social media has the ability to offer access, but that access is a two-way street. It's strange to meet people who say they are a fan of my work, or who act like they know things about me simply because they follow me on Twitter. It's weird to sometimes feel so exposed, but I'm determined to use my platform to be my authentic self. If you follow me and not just BGHC on Twitter, you'll come to find out that I am nuanced and imperfect, funny and weird, smart and sad. I am a hockey fan and I am Black. I am a writer and a fangirl, and all these things can be true at the same time. To reveal these variations means remaining vulnerable, transparent, and fallible, so that people can see their stories reflected in mine. Telling my own story is actually quite terrifying, if I'm being honest, but it's also exhilarating and life-changing and so, so worth it.

Organizations like Black Girl Hockey Club exist to give marginalized folks control over our narratives. Within these spaces, we are able to authentically enjoy hockey on our own terms, because we clearly delineate the issues that affect our communities and share that information using whatever agency we have. But Black women are not here to save society from itself. So-called allies who support equity only when it is trendy to do so are encouraged to facilitate inclusive leadership modalities or discontinue taking up space in a movement that does not centre white people. For Black queer femmes in particular, the work toward equity is a lived experience that does not end when Black Lives Matter stops trending or June's Pride celebrations are over.

In hockey, there are few who do it bigger or badder for The Culture than Kim Davis. While Black fans may be critical of the power structures within the NHL, we are all aware of the doors Ms. Davis had to break down in order to get to the position she currently has in the league. As Senior Executive Vice President of Social Impact, Growth Initiatives and Legislative Affairs, she holds the highest executive position of any Black person in the NHL, and she does so with a keen understanding of the depth of her responsibility in that space. In fact, when I ask her what her title is, she gently chastises me, saying, "I describe the work that I do, as opposed to the title that I hold," and then goes on to tell me about that work in detail.

"So I have responsibility for, well, a number of things," she begins. "One is how do we build new and enhance existing relationships with growth markets defined as racialized groups, gender groups, LGBT groups, and others that have felt either marginalized or underrepresented in the sport of hockey.

"Looking at those audiences through the lens of growth versus the lens of charity, I have responsibility for the NHL Foundation and the dissemination of the funds from the foundation and building the foundation. I have responsibility for the Industry Growth Fund, which is a partnership between the league and the Players' Association, to grow hockey across

North America at the youth level. I have responsibility for multicultural marketing, and all of our legislative affairs.

"I joined the NHL in December of 2017 . . . and my first experience was meeting the Board of Governors—the owners and the governors of the sport. It was quite something because, while over my thirty-plus-year career I had been in many, many board roles where I was the only one [who was] both female *and* [a] woman of colour, there had been few experiences in the past ten to fifteen years where I went into a room that was virtually all white men, a hundred, a hundred-plus, who were all governors, and that was quite, quite stunning for me.

"My experience with the NHL actually started a year before I [officially] joined, when I was a consultant. The intent of the work [at the time] was to help the NHL think about how to put together their marketing principles and how to think about organizing all of their marketing assets.

"I met the commissioner [Gary Bettman]. I was *interviewing* the commissioner. And we had some very direct and delicate conversations where, you know, he didn't necessarily agree with me and I didn't agree with him. I felt like, in many ways, he probably had not experienced anyone being as direct and pushing back as directly as I had on some of his theses around the ways in which multicultural markets should be marketed to and thought about.

"I actually think maybe it was refreshing for him to have a different perspective and to look at the work ahead through a different lens. I also think it was an opportune moment, the league had just celebrated its centennial and really taken a well-deserved victory lap around the way the sport had grown. The expansion of teams, the speed on the ice, the progress being made about the sport being perceived as a, you know, a 'fighting sport' to one that was much more strategic. So a lot of great things to celebrate, but still some real challenges in terms of how communities of colour and others felt about the sense of welcome and engagement within the sport, and I'm not sure that anyone knew how to tackle that problem.

"I think it's probably just this year [2021] where people have gotten used to and comfortable with the fact that there's a Black woman in a senior position in hockey and that it's not performative. Like, *she actually has some power and people listen to her. And she matters, right?*"

With Kim Davis and her team—people like Jeff Scott, Kwame Mason, and Melissa Parnagian—at the helm of the NHL's Hockey Is For Everyone initiative, what is arguably the world's most prominent hockey organization has the opportunity to change the narrative of Black folks in hockey. Respectfully, Ms. Davis knows exactly what she's doing by hiring BIPOC executives and placing them in positions of power throughout the league. They will be the ones to tell the story of how Black folks engage with hockey as fans, players, executives, and at all levels of the game. While the NHL is far from perfect, Kim Davis is committed to doing what she can to change things from the inside of one of hockey's most important institutions. While it sometimes seems like the policies, the committees, and the changes aren't moving fast enough, marginalized fans have to remember that the NHL is an institution created by white people for white people. Conn Smythe and Bobby Orr and Don Cherry all remind us of that fact. The story of Black folks in hockey hasn't been told yet, at least not by Black people. But that's where Kim Davis, Dr. Razack, and even this book come in.

"Storytelling is so critically important to communities of colour," Ms. Davis says. "Because we never had our true stories told in the mainstream, we typically are telling our stories to each other, and affirming each other as opposed to changing the narrative of how other communities see us.

"And so what happens is, you know, and Spike Lee has said this over many, many years, that if you leave it up to someone else to curate your narrative, then they're going to tell the story through their lens and not through yours. And he's so absolutely right about that. Because what happens is the stories that are told *about us* as opposed to *by us* are typically the 'flash cards,' as my son who's an anthropologist refers to them, and it's those narratives and those biases that sit in the world around us. And so if we don't change that narrative, then it continues to get reinforced in the mainstream and that's who we are, and they don't see anything else.

"That's why storytelling is so important, and that's why integrating storytelling into the mainstream is so important. This is one of the things that I spend, literally, almost every waking hour doing. I mean, the things that people don't see and know about what I do is [that I am] constantly educating and helping my colleagues in every aspect of our business [to] understand who we are as communities, and [to] give them access to [our] stories so that it reframes their sense of our flash cards. Just talking about what this movement means and sharing data with them that reframes their understanding of who we are. For example, we have forty-six BIPOC players on the roster today, we don't have to keep showcasing the same three BIPOC players over and over and over again, let's showcase these forty-six. Twenty-nine of those forty-six are Black, [and] there's another forty-six that are in the system that can be called up at any time. That's ninety-two right there. And then there's another twenty free agents.

"Every time I talk to an audience of influence about this, who are typically whites, they're shocked, because everybody thinks there are like five BIPOC. So unless we're showing that on the screen, unless we're showing that on our sizzle reels, unless we're panning the stadiums and showing the fanbase, unless that's in the mainstream—not some diversity clip but in the mainstream of everything that is hockey—we are not going to change that flash card."

In order to shift the stereotypes about marginalized folks, particularly in hockey, we must be the ones to tell our own stories. For Dr. Sabrina Razack, the connection between organizations such as BGHC and historically Black feminist movements creates an opportunity to upend the status quo and rebuild the broken system that is professional hockey. In her work she tells the story of the legacy of Black women in sports while placing Black Girl Hockey Club on a historical timeline of social justice activism that includes Audre Lorde and Fannie Lou Hamer. No pressure! Kim Davis, on the other hand, recognizes that her main responsibility lies in telling the stories of Black communities in hockey to the traditional audience of the NHL—white people. She is determined to bring the untold narratives of marginalized folks in hockey to the forefront of the National Hockey League's marketing strategy. To do so, she has built a team of diverse hockey executives to strategically execute an internal plan of action that will be her own legacy within the historical hockey organization. Together, these strategies have a profound impact on the sport, as others will become inspired to do their own activism because of the representation they see at the highest levels, while also gaining access to hockey spaces through the grassroots and viral work of Black Girl Hockey Club.

Dr. Courtney Szto also believes that projects such as Dr. Razack's examination of Black Girl Hockey Club as a sports media space reveal the power that social media gives marginalized communities to tell their own stories. It gives anti-racism activists in sports an entry point. "Social media has probably been the most beneficial technology that we've seen in the last few decades," she tells me. "For marginalized communities, I really don't think that there has been anything like it since the invention of the zine, right? Where people can write themselves into existence, and write themselves into the cultural narrative.

"We might still be kind of geographically dispersed, but we can connect and fit into a much larger narrative that we haven't seen in the mainstream hockey culture. And I think what I try to impress when I talk to hockey groups is like, they always talk about how hockey's so expensive, hockey's so racist, whatever, it's the worst. But there's Black Girl Hockey Club, and there's also Black Girls Surf, there's Black Girls Run, Black Girls Do Bike, Brown Girls Climb. Women in particular are galvanizing in various communities, because they've never been included. So I think, and that's really thanks to social media, that we can do this from different corners of the continent."

It is through the social media presence of people like Dr. Szto, Shireen Ahmed, Erica Ayala, and Jashvina Shah that I myself came to know about the anti-racism work happening in sports as I tried to figure out how to best use my skills to elevate Black women in this space. As I am writing this, the Black Girl Hockey Club Twitter account has more than 30k followers. Our Instagram has over 10k. Launched in 2019, these accounts are clearing houses of information on race, social justice, and hockey, with followers from all over the world. The international reach of social media gives BGHC the opportunity to engage with foreign media—such as an interview I did in 2021 with *Süddeutsche Zeitung*, one of the largest daily newspapers in Germany, and the podcast BGHC board member Fatou Bah recorded with a hockey fan out of Brazil. Social media is a place to find people who share similar interests and to develop community. When I come across racialized scholars and journalists discussing anti-racism in hockey on my timeline, it shows me and others that there are people doing the work out loud in these spaces. It makes an organization like Black Girl Hockey Club not such a far-fetched idea after all, and if we can be an inspiration, even better.

Dr. Szto reiterates how important a curated and thoughtful social media space can be to racialized women and co-conspirators working toward anti-racism in sports. Social media is how she and I found each other, how we both continue to communicate with followers all over the world, and how we allow the world to see us. We are hockey fans, but we are also multifaceted, with real feelings around real issues.

BGHC started on social media, with a group of women of colour and our friends who all just wanted to find a space to belong. With access to TikTok, Twitter, Instagram, and even Facebook, advocacy movements have the opportunity to form organically across the world. Folks with similar values and interests can find each other, no matter where they live. This is why social media poses such a danger to those who would prefer that marginalized communities not galvanize but instead remain disconnected and unaware that white supremacy and capitalism have their foot on all our necks.

While Black women are creating a new narrative and changing the way that we as a community engage in the hockey space with intention, confidence, and swagger, there is harm in believing that we do not feel sadness, depression, anxiety, hopelessness, or fear. Black women are not meant to be strong all the time. Sometimes we are sad, sometimes we are scared, and sometimes we harbour righteous anger that society deems too much, too loud, or too aggressive. While archetypes are an easy way to categorize literary characters and to find the universal themes in narrative tropes, *real* people deserve to express nuance. Black women deserve to manifest the entire spectrum of emotions without fear of being categorized and written off, and we deserve a safe space to do this in, no matter what industry we work in or what position we occupy. Society as a whole frowns on Black women engaging fully with our emotions. We cannot give ourselves over to them as white women do; we must mute our sadness, our elation, our anger, in order to be socially acceptable. If we are lucky, we are in homes and families that encourage expressing a range of emotions, but often Black folks are taught to suppress ourselves for our own good and safety. We don't get to make mistakes—and if we do, we should be prepared to face violence in various forms for our misunderstanding. It's a lesson you don't want to learn the hard way.

Tembe Denton-Hurst, a writer at *The Strategist* covering beauty and books, penned this in a 2023 article in *The Cut*: "There are sacrifices associated with navigating well enough to get to the top. You lose some of yourself in all of that. Even if they hired you to come in swinging, eventually they'll expect you to curve your back to the shape of the institution. It is the way these systems are designed." Even though Black women acutely feel this double standard, there are marginalized folks at all levels of hockey who are affecting institutional infrastructure and generally shaking up our corners of the sport by remaining our authentic selves—wary, but not turned away by the unrealistic expectations imposed on BIPOC leaders. While women like Kim Davis have been lauded as "saviours" of the anti-racism movement in hockey, Black women are not here to save your favourite sport. We defer to a horizontal power structure while focusing on persuading others to join a common cause, uplifting peers, and supporting marginalized communities in order to build solid infrastructures reflecting the inclusive values of Black feminism. We do this because we need community as much as anyone else.

Sports scholars like Dr. Courtney Szto and Dr. Sabrina Razack emphasize the importance of building our own spaces, narratives, and policies, while creating a framework of understanding around activism in sports using quantifiable data and scholarly research. With organizations such as Black Girl

Hockey Club acting as clearing houses of information and providing access to the game in a variety of ways for Black athletes and our allies, we are subverting stereotypes, telling our own stories, and making our own way.

BLACKNESS IS A GIFT I CAN GIVE HER

When Kelsey Koelzer, former professional ice hockey player for the NWHL's Metropolitan Riveters and the first Black woman to coach NCAA women's hockey, tells me that, as a biracial woman, she feels like a "bridge" between Black and white folks, I recognize the duality in such a statement immediately. Personally, I love bridges. They are beautiful, powerful structures. They pepper the landscape of Pittsburgh, one of my favourite cities in the United States—and not just because of its hockey team. Bridges are durable and strong, spanning distances with a purpose. Without bridges, communities would remain static and isolated, never growing or expanding to shift with the times. The thing about bridges: we often don't think about them until they collapse under the weight of too much pressure. We use bridges for our own ends, barely considering the limitations of said bridge. But if a bridge is not maintained, secured, and taken care of by the communities it binds, the bridge becomes unstable, unsteady, and unreliable.

When Kelsey, a biracial woman of European and African heritage, encounters an intersection of misogyny and racism within the precarious space she occupies in between cultures, she chooses to bridge that gap using education, consistency, and a whole lot of patience. As a biracial woman myself, I too often feel like I exist in the spaces in between Black and white cultures. I can't control other people's perception of me, but that doesn't mean I'm unaware of the impact that my high-yellow, light skin has on Black communities, or the impact the existence of multiracial folks like me has on white supremacist ideological narratives. It's not comfortable for me to acknowledge that even though I pioneered an organization like Black Girl Hockey Club—which is focused on creating equity in hockey for Black women—I do so with the privilege of my proximity to whiteness. My whiteness is a part of me as much as my Blackness is, and I will sit in the shame that comes with recognizing white privilege and then do what I can to subvert the systems that offer me what they don't offer my dark-skinned sisters, because I love Black folks. I will continue to make choices that uplift Black folks, not only because of my heritage but because the history of Black people in America is one of inequity, and if I can make a positive impact on the world that benefits Black women, I'm going to do it.

I didn't start out planning to talk about biraciality—mine or anyone else's—and yet, as my conversations with Kelsey continue, I realize that multiracialism, colourism, and the white gaze are all subjects that need to be addressed, even in hockey. Kelsey lives just outside of Philadelphia and has been playing ice hockey since she was four. She is light-skinned with soft, straight (heat-pressed?) hair flowing down her back. Her mother is white and her father is Black. When I ask her about race, Kelsey tells me she is "mixed," which, throughout history, has in itself been fraught with trauma. Although both Kelsey and I come from loving, multicultural families, America's history, specifically with miscegenation, is dark (no pun intended). In the antebellum South, a person with African ancestry and no European ancestry was considered "Negro," while a "mulatto" was a child of mixed African and European ancestry—often the product of rape or seduction, and the sexual appetites of powerful white men. In his 1918 book *The Mulatto in the United States*, Edward Byron Reuter defined *mulatto* as "all those members of the Negro race with a visible admixture of white blood. Thus used, the word is a general term to include all Negroes of mixed ancestry regardless of the degree of intermixture." During the eighteenth and nineteenth centuries, particular terms were used to describe free Negroes based on complexion and physical characteristics rather than proof of ancestry. According to Brooke Bergan's *Storyville: A Hidden Mirror*, historical terminology for race designated that

A mulatto was the child of a white and a Negro;
a quadroon, of a white and a mulatto;
an octoroon, of a white and a quadroon;
a *griffe*, of a Negro and a mulatto;
a *maraban*, of a mulatto and a *griffe*;
a *sacatra*, of a quadroon and a *griffe*;
metis, meamelouc, sang-mele, os rouge
—one day her child might pass *a blanc*.

Interracial marriage was only ratified into law with the 1967 Supreme Court decision *Loving v. Virginia*, which decreed all state anti-miscegenation laws unconstitutional. According to the 2020 U.S. census, the multiracial population in the United States has increased by 276 per cent since 2010. With more multiracial births comes a greater number of children born with varying skin tones. Having light skin creates a proximity to whiteness that produces a false hierarchy in socio-political structures in America and across the globe.

Colourism projects anti-Blackness into our own communities, measuring beauty using methods such as the "paper bag test," a practice in which an individual's skin tone is compared to the colour of a brown paper bag, to discriminate against anyone darker than the paper. Colourism is an uncomfortable topic, particularly in Black communities, because it is born of racism and white supremacy. It is rooted in prejudices based on skin tone, with the darkest skin associated with archetypes of evil, uncleanliness, and darkness, and the palest white skin associated with goodness, purity, and light. In her book *Hood Feminism*, Mikki Kendall discusses in depth the damaging effect of colourism on Black culture. She reminds readers that colourism isn't just about beauty aesthetics and personal preference. Colourism is tied to lower employment and marriage rates, higher arrest rates, and longer prison sentences. In stories like Toni Morrison's 1970 novel *The Bluest Eye*, the light eyes, pale skin, and delicate features of white women are uplifted as societal beauty standards, and the wide noses, hips, and lips of Black women remain oversexualized while simultaneously being considered unattractive. Even as white women profit from stealing style and speech from Black culture, even as they change their body shapes to emulate Black women, the features of white women are considered the measure of beauty. Everything else is a fad.

The act of a light-skinned person of African heritage engaging with the public as white is called "passing," and there are numerous books and films that deal with the topic, created by both Black and white artists. The first time I ever encountered the concept in art was in the 1934 film *Imitation of Life*, directed by John M. Stahl. Apparently, Stahl was adamant about hiring a white-passing Black actress to play the role of Peola, a white-passing Black character—as opposed to hiring a white actress, which would have been deemed acceptable in Hollywood at the time. In *Imitation of Life*, Peola is the white-passing daughter of Delilah Johnson, a subservient, mammy-like character played by Louise Beavers, a dark-skinned actress who had previously been cast to play stereotypical "slave" or "maid" roles in early twentieth-century film and television. For Peola, Stahl hired Fredi Washington, "the Black girl with the green eyes"—a dancer for Josephine Baker who had also acted on Broadway with Paul Robeson during the Harlem Renaissance. Both of her parents were of mixed African and European descent, but Fredi had always been told she could work abroad and "pass" as French, avoiding the heartaches of being Black in America if only she would hide her heritage.

In 1937, Washington co-founded the Negro Actors Guild of America (NAG), and in 1945 she spoke of the phenomenon of "passing" to Earl Conrad, a white journalist for the New York bureau of the *Chicago Defender*. In response to questions on why she refused to pretend to be white, even after being told by Hollywood producers that she would receive more opportunities if she "passed," Washington told Conrad, "You see I'm a mighty proud gal, and I can't for the life of me find any valid reason why anyone should lie about their origin, or anything else for that matter. Frankly, I do not ascribe to the stupid theory of white supremacy and to try to hide the fact that I am a Negro for economic or any other reasons. If I do, I would be agreeing [that] to be a Negro makes me inferior and that I have swallowed whole hog all of the propaganda dished out by our fascist-minded white citizens." Washington refused to hate any part of herself, and used her privilege to organize within her community, pioneering a way for Black actors through the formation of NAG. She moved with intentionality and chose her own path, regardless of any assumptions and preconceived notions about her—unlike Peola, the character she played in *Imitation of Life*. Through a deliberate and steadfast commitment to honour herself, her heritage, and her community, Fredi Washington was able to create a space in Hollywood for Black actors because she loved Black people.

I spent much of my youth confused and searching for an identity, a culture. As the biracial child of a white single mother, I grew up around her people. White people. My Black father, Henry, moved back to the East Coast of the United States after he and my mother, Rebecca, divorced, right around the time I started kindergarten in California. My father wasn't a permanent fixture in my life—I didn't have access to him or to his side of the family. My mother loved me, but she could not teach me to be Black. Instead, she taught me to ask questions, to be open-minded, and offered me the opportunity to build relationships with Black women in our community. I stumbled into my twenties trying to figure out how to navigate life as a

Black woman, even though I was raised by white people, went to white schools, and had mostly white friends. When I brought up my Blackness in these spaces, I was assured that my race "didn't matter" and that my non-Black teachers and friends "didn't see colour." When I was a child, those statements seemed like reassurances, safe and without judgement. As I grew older, I began to recognize how this ideology erased my Blackness. In order for me to maintain my own mental health and well-being, I require the folks I keep around me to not just acknowledge but also care deeply about my intersectional identity and the social impact of issues surrounding gender, race, sexuality, and ability. I need those around me to care about Black culture, or else there is a huge part of me that they will never engage with—and what's the point in that?

When I gave birth to my only child in 2002, I contemplated how my own broken family tree and lack of Black elders might affect the way my daughter engaged with her cultural identity. Even at the time that she was born and I became a mother myself, I did not know how to be my father's daughter. Henry had come back into my life in 1996, when I was seventeen years old, and I was angry. It wasn't until I had my own child that I began to let go of the deep resentment I felt toward my father for not being around. My sisters, my mothers, and my daughter acted as a balm to the relationship. These women helped heal me. My sister Sarah and my mother Rebecca model for me what it is to forgive my father and let go of a troubled past. My sisters from different mothers, Jazzmun and Samantha, remind me how much there is to love in our father. My stepmother, Cathy, makes sure to let me know that, as Black women, we have a responsibility to model inclusive behaviour for the little Black girls who watch and learn from their elders, as I learn from Cathy. We teach, learn, and mend together.

If it weren't for these women, my father and I might never have been able to heal the wounds of the past and learn to love one another again. When I became a parent, I needed the hurt and abandonment that disconnected me from my roots not to sever my daughter's relationship with our culture. Henry is the patriarch of the family, but it wasn't always that way. My father is a difficult man, but I love him. He continues to model for me what it means to be Black in America, from his mistakes to his triumphs, and I continue to learn from his perspective.

The world teaches all Black folks, regardless of skin tone, that we are better off disassociating from our Blackness. In America, our Blackness can literally kill us. It can be terrifying to be Black here, knowing that we cannot go to church, or to the grocery store, or jog down the road without the possibility of being murdered simply for being Black, and that the police are part of the problem. There are Black folks out there without the best interests of Black folks in mind, preferring to cater to white supremacy and reap the benefits of broken systems. In his 1903 essay "The Talented Tenth" in *The Negro Problem*, W.E.B. Du Bois addressed the effects of white supremacy on Black folks by reminding readers that "for three long centuries this people lynched Negroes who dared to be brave, raped black women who dared to be virtuous, crushed dark-hued youth who dared to be ambitious, and encouraged and made to flourish servility and lewdness and apathy." In the twenty-first century, gun violence and drug use in low-income Black communities, the lack of Black wealth and home ownership, and the high Black prison population can all be traced back to institutional policies meant to subjugate and oppress Black Americans.

There are also specific effects of white supremacy on Black women, as discussed in 1989 by UCLA and Columbia Law School professor Kimberlé Crenshaw in her *University of Chicago Legal Forum* academic article "Demarginalizing the Intersection of Race and Sex: A Black Feminist Critique of Antidiscrimination Doctrine, Feminist Theory and Antiracist Politics." In this key text, Crenshaw accounts for the intersecting effects of race, gender, and class, as well as the specific oppression faced by Black women. Her work has helped shape Critical Race Theory in the American and South African legal systems for more than twenty years, and she is acknowledged as the first scholar to define and utilize the theory of intersectionality. As Crenshaw tells us: "These problems of exclusion cannot be solved simply by including Black women within an already established analytical structure . . . for feminist theory and antiracist policy discourse to embrace the experiences and concerns of Black women, the entire framework that has been used as a basis for translating 'women's experience' or 'the Black experience' into concrete policy demands must be rethought and recast."

While I work to navigate my Black intersectional identity, I understand that to be of service to my community, I must recognize the fact that the primarily white institute (PWI) I graduated from and work for offers me a measure of educational and class privilege. I have to acknowledge that many of my hobbies (hockey, sci-fi nerdery) are associated with whiteness. I have to realize the daily advantages of walking through the world with mocha-coloured skin and soft 3C curls and the ability to code-switch. I have to admit that I easily engage in "double consciousness" and infiltrate white spaces. If I forget to examine the advantages that white supremacy offers me, I can easily succumb to the hubris that goes hand in hand with societal standards built on anti-Blackness. I can fall into the trap of becoming the "only one" in the room. I might even start to enjoy being a "model minority," representing an entire culture for non-Black folks. Unfortunately, when my Blackness becomes a problem, when I consider pushing back against harmful institutional policy, I am unlikely to succeed without additional representation and community support. This is why community is so important. In the spaces I currently occupy, it is my goal to use social capital to amplify the voices, businesses, and visions of Black folks, while gaining the knowledge and resources needed to build sustainable spaces with Black leadership. As the mother of a biracial daughter who can "pass," I recognize that the onus is on me to teach my daughter how to intentionally interact with her Blackness, as well as educate her on privilege. I can teach her how the past continues to impact and enrich our everyday experiences. Blackness is a gift I can give her.

These are the lessons I must teach my daughter, and the lessons that women like Kelsey Koelzer are passing on to the next generation of hockey players. For Kelsey, recognizing her privilege means using it to educate players while growing the game of hockey. She coaches at Arcadia University, a PWI, with a team of all-white players. Over video chat on a sunny summer morning, Kelsey talks to me about how she navigates her job as coach while being one of the few Black leaders on campus, and the task of talking about race.

"I have this awesome audience of young people that are so excited, and I have fellow coaches that are really supportive, but at the same time don't necessarily know how to always lead these conversations. I've had the opportunity to speak with a couple of teams about how they can change their actions to be more inclusive and more supportive of their minority teammates."

She goes on to discuss the importance of diversifying at the college level, in order to create a more melanated pipeline to professional hockey. "You know, minority students come for a visit, and sometimes they're going to a campus that's primarily a white campus. If [minority students] are going into a primarily white team, these young [non-minority] people need to be equipped on how to create the most accepting and accessible space for these minority recruits coming in so that we can make our sport, at a higher level, more diverse.

"Joining different task forces on campus has been really important for me in the last year. Specifically, targeting how [Arcadia University can] increase enrolment among minorities and especially how we do that within our athletic programs. By being intentional, I think other people realize that they need to be intentional."

In 2019, Kelsey was named to the NHL and NHLPA Female Hockey Advisory Committee, which is dedicated to accelerating the growth of women's hockey in North America while also ensuring more women and girls have opportunities to experience the benefits the sport offers. In 2020, she began working with the National Women's Hockey League (NWHL), later the Premier Hockey Federation (PHF), as Advisor to the Commissioner on Diversity, Equity, and Inclusion. In this role, she consulted with then league commissioner Tyler Tumminia to "build a cultural awareness" within the league and to design strategic plans to encourage inclusivity.

Both of these were unpaid positions that involved Kelsey sharing her expertise and experiences with the organizations so that they could better develop equitable policies for marginalized folks. While professional hockey leagues consider these inclusive roles and committees a step in the right direction, the lack of equitable pay is indicative of a larger problem that stems from classism and is, ultimately, steeped in racism. What about those of us who cannot afford to work for free? Is there a space for us in these organizations?

Kelsey believes giving her time and energy for free is worth it for the difference she is making in the hockey community. "I don't think that having it become a paid position is out of the question. Yeah, I was willing to do it. It's me having conversations with hockey people. If I can tell my story and it helps a little, then so be it."

While Kelsey has the privilege to be able to work for free, Black women shouldn't feel ashamed to ask these institutions to pay them what they are worth. During the 2021–22 hockey season, Black Girl Hockey Club launched the campaign "Get Uncomfortable in the Workplace," focusing on issues of equity in the workplace, specifically for Black and racialized women. With the success of the 2020 Get Uncomfortable Pledge to "Encourage, Employ, and Educate" across the National Hockey League, and signatories like the Los Angeles

Kings, Pittsburgh Penguins, Toronto Maple Leafs, Seattle Kraken, and others supporting the BGHC mission, we are pushing clubs to discuss topics like the wage gap and hiring practices in order to create paid positions for Black women. In panel events moderated by women of colour working in sports media, such as Erica Ayala (Black Rosie Media), Shireen Ahmed (CBC), and Dr. Tunisha Singleton (BGHC board president and media specialist), we formulate guidelines and best practices and share them internally within the clubs as well as externally with fans and season ticket holders.

As someone who comes from a family of educators and who has taught for almost twenty years at expensive, private educational institutions, I am a firm believer in the importance of lifelong education as well as free education for all. The vision for BGHC includes just that. All online panel discussions have multiple payment options, from "free" to a donation of the giver's choice. I love a handout, and so we often create a tangible takeaway for BGHC online or in-person events, with specific information as well as more general guidelines around advocacy in hockey. It's within these events, especially in person, that community bonds are forged. We encourage co-conspirators to support Black peers and employees by advocating for them in the workplace, even when we are not in the room. Black Girl Hockey Club is committed to uplifting Black women at all levels of hockey, from the ice to the boardroom and everywhere in between. The Get Uncomfortable Campaign asks signatories of the pledge, from individuals to teams to leagues, to hold the difficult conversations around the topics of race and hockey, and then to make the difficult choices in order to create a safer environment for Black women in our institutions, including hockey. These difficult choices include re-examining hiring practices, creating hiring quotas, recruiting at HBCUs and other Black organizations, offering paid internships, and creating diversity committees in-house with the actual power to facilitate change.

Ironically, it's difficult for BGHC to get folks to pay us to do this work. Contrary to popular belief, we don't have a large grant or donor at this point that we can count on to help keep the lights on and the intersectional education flowing. BGHC has always thrived on the support of individual donors and clubs who believe in the cause. In the U.S., BGHC subsists more on grassroots fundraising than corporate support. It's not what I expected when I started this business, but it is indicative of how difficult it really is to have these types of conversations.

For Kelsey, her induction into the Black Girl Hockey Club space came at the very beginning. She chose to support this work before BGHC filed for non-profit status or had any sort of professional reputation around ice hockey. Moving with meaning, Kelsey continues to offer her effort and enthusiasm to help advance the mission of Black Girl Hockey Club, and we are working together to use our privilege to help other Black women gain access to hockey spaces. I remember vividly the first BGHC meet-up in Washington, DC, back in December 2018, and the time I got to spend with Kelsey and her mother, Kristine Koelzer. Together with a few others, we enjoyed a pre-game meal and a quick trip to the National Portrait Gallery to see the Michelle and Barack Obama portraits, by Amy Sherald and Kehinde Wiley respectively. As our group made its way through the gallery to see the Obamas and other works, I noticed Kelsey and Kristine sitting shoulder to shoulder, staring in silence at a large landscape. The image of the two of them, mother and daughter, sharing space while having two very different experiences within the world stays with me even now and reminds me of the camaraderie that I share with my own mother. It reminds me that my mom has always wanted the best for me, and that she continues to encourage me to chase joy and covet peace above all else. I am reminded of the long drives to singing performances in high school, and the ways my mom supports me still, pushing me to be my best while acknowledging that she doesn't fully understand my experiences around race and never really will. When it comes to Black culture and the issues that I face as a Black woman, she won't *ever* fully understand those parts of me or my sister, her daughters, whom she raised on her own from the age of twenty-two.

For Kelsey, the support of her non-Black family members helped guide her to hockey, despite their different experiences. "What really sparked hockey for me and really for our family was my two older cousins. It was a whole family thing. My aunt did the heat press for all the jersey decals for the entire team at the rink, my uncle coached a couple of different teams and my two older cousins played ice hockey from a very young age, and my mom would always go. We were a very close family so she would just bring me along to their games. She developed a relationship with the rink as well and started working there. She managed the snack bar, and once I started skating and playing, she managed our leagues and all that kind of stuff."

Still, Kelsey understands that even as she attempts to bridge a cultural gap between Black and white folks in hockey, her proximity to whiteness will never fully grant her access to white culture. "My entire family that I grew up with is all white, so I see it from both sides. I was raised by a white family. I understand that culture and the sport and what they're used to. But also, I am who I am, and I look completely different from everyone in my family, and I look completely different from everyone else in the sport, and there's a good reason for that. And I want to also intentionally use that to try to push for a change. So, I definitely am intentional. And I'm trying to . . . bridge that platform, whether people actually listen that way or not.

"I could talk as much as I want about my upbringing, but the fact is, I don't look like them and I don't look like the people I'm trying to get through to. The fact that I was raised by a white family does not protect me from ridicule."

It's eye-opening to grow up and realize that there is inherent racism underlying all of our institutions—educational, carceral, financial, sports. It can feel overwhelming and stressful and emotional. As a Black woman, I cannot imagine the privilege that comes with just *existing* as white. But one of the hardest realizations I've had is that the white people I love can—and do—not only recognize but *exercise* their ability to opt out of feeling the fear and anger that develop when we closely examine the infrastructures of our society and recognize the tactics implicit in gatekeeping access and power within these institutions. It is a stark reality that many of the white people I care about consistently utilize their option to say, "I don't *feel* like talking about race, gender, ability, or sexuality," even as people are murdered because of the intersections they occupy. Even more difficult is knowing there are marginalized communities who buy into the bullshit system as well. This objection to the realities of inequity only reiterates that marginalized folks are meant to sit down, be quiet, and not make folks uncomfortable over institutions they have "no control" over. Which, of course, perpetuates a cycle of exclusion, trauma, and abuse within these systems. Watch whiteness work! See how it regulates history, hiring practices, even hockey. How it tells us to be content with the crumbs we are given, to never ask questions, never expect an explanation of whiteness because the bar is always moving.

Colourism is whiteness at work within Black communities. There's no denying the connection between colourism and palatability to white hockey culture. In hockey, a number of the most visible Black players and fans are biracial. Sarah Nurse. Blake Bolden. Saroya Tinker. Kelsey Koelzer. Me. All biracial. All working toward creating community for other Black women in hockey. What does this phenomenon mean for the movement? Is Black hockey culture being co-opted by light-skinned girls with 3C hair? The short answer is "no"; however, reality is more complicated than that. I and these other light-skinned queens do engage Black communities with intentionality, but we also cannot forget how colourism influences and affects our opportunities. How the media, our institutions, and society as a whole go out of their way to remind us that proximity to Blackness means death and that the best thing to do is submit to white supremacy and European standards. My light-skinned siblings! We are not to perpetuate myths of white supremacy or associate dark skin with anything but beauty, opulence, and glory! It's the melanin for me! Light-skinned queens, we must realize our proximity to whiteness does not define us, nor does it make us better (or worse) than anyone else. We must commit to learning from the vast variety within the Black experience, and if we make mistakes, commit to sitting in the feeling of being wrong. Let the richness of the Black experience become a balm when the world wounds you. Use your privilege to amplify all Black voices, and commit to moving with purpose within marginalized communities. Be a bridge to something better, and take care of the bridges in your own communities.

Three Times I Saw a Hockey Game in Pittsburgh and One Time I Didn't

i.

The Black hockey network is very small, and the Black-women-in-hockey network is even smaller. To my sheer delight, in 2019, my beloved Penguins hired two amazing Black women named Tracey McCants Lewis and Delvina Morrow. Tracey, Delvina, and I took six months to do it, but we planned our dream Black Girl Hockey Club meet-up, and when we got together in Pittsburgh at the end of January 2020, it was with a sense of joy and accomplishment for what had come to fruition after all our hard work. The event lasted two days, with a Friday morning ball hockey game with the kiddos at Miller Elementary, an evening hockey game at PPG Paints Arena, and a screening of Kwame Mason's *Soul on Ice* and a panel discussion at the August Wilson African American Cultural Center in downtown Pittsburgh. I enjoyed all of the activities, and always look back on this event as an example of how a hockey team can engage with local marginalized communities in a unique and authentic way. I might be biased, obviously, but it was pretty great, nonetheless.

There's ample footage from this weekend, because I had the Penguins' (Emmy Award–winning) production team and a camera crew from NBC following me around on game day, but there's one moment missing from the sizzle reels that I will remember forever. I had brought my homemade "Geno Is Fire" sign with me all the way from California, and there I was, stuck doing pre-game media scrums, sign in hand, when all I really wanted was to get down to the glass and let Penguins alternate captain, hockey superstar, and my fave, Evgeni "Geno" Malkin, know I was there to cheer him on! Suddenly, I saw a chance to break away. A classic introvert move—leaving without saying goodbye! I scampered (quickly, for a big girl) down to the lower bowl area, just steps away from the professionals, Geno sign in hand, friends in tow, and a camera crew scrambling to catch up as I tried to lose them so I could fangirl in peace! Squeezed in between my amazing friends Christy and Amanda and a few hundred Pens fans, I shook my sign at Geno, and cheered as the boys swarmed the ice, preparing to win me my first home game with an overtime goal from captain Sidney Crosby himself. There's no footage of *that* on the internet.

ii.

The second time I saw a Pens game in Pittsburgh, Geno walked right by the open door of our suite but I was in the bathroom being anti-social and I missed it! In the fall of 2021, Delvina Morrow invited me to join a group of local Black, brown, and

LGBTQ folks in a suite at PPG Paints Arena to see the Penguins play the Dallas Stars. That's right! My two favourite hockey teams, playing against each other, and a chance to hang with my people. I had to go! So, I set up a couple of meetings with local hockey folks as an excuse to be in town longer, and travelled to Pittsburgh the week of my forty-first birthday. That week, I walked across the vibrant yellow bridges listening to Mac Miller, scribbled in my journal on park benches overlooking the Ohio River, and ate lunch with friends at their favourite food spots.

At the game, though, I didn't know a soul except Delvina and Tracey, who were obviously working, and so my introverted self ended up taking a breather in the bathroom right at the exact time that Evgeni Malkin strode by our door on his way to Mario Lemieux's suite for a photo op, just around the corner. When I returned to the suite after doing some breathing exercises in the bathroom stall and taking a few selfies, both Tracey and Delvina rushed over to tell me what I had missed. He'd walked right by! Everyone saw but me! I even received text messages from people watching the broadcast live, asking if I'd seen Geno at the game! No, ma'am, I did not, because my stupid introverted ass was busy hiding in the bathroom.

Take that as a warning, introverts. Don't let the bathroom selfie sabotage your dreams!

iii.

The third time I saw the Penguins play a home game in Pittsburgh was the day before my forty-first birthday. Yeah, I saw the Pens play twice in the same week. It's a thing I do sometimes! Anyway, that same week that Geno and I had passed each other like ships in the night (he was out for half of that season with an injury), I saw the Pens play again, this time with a small group of local BGHC friends. Going to a game with BGHC just feels different, and the vibes that night were immaculate. I didn't have to do any interviews, there were no camera crews, it was just me and the homies, watching our favourite flightless birds win a hockey game. Everyone knows that BGHC has a pretty good track record of wins when we're in-house. I'm not saying that anti-racism and equitable, community-based engagement makes winning hockey teams, but I'm not NOT saying that, either.

As I walked back to my downtown hotel after the win with other Pens fans in a sea of black and yellow, I couldn't help feeling that, at that moment, my time as a Pittsburgh Penguins fan had come full circle. Ten years ago, the Penguins had sparked my interest in a sport that would end up changing my life. It all started on these streets, with these colours, and this team—and god, am I glad it did.

iv.

As an English major, I am obviously a huge nerd. In grad school, I was the queen of the nerds for a time—a.k.a. acting president of the La Sierra University chapter of the international English honour society Sigma Tau Delta. Every year, ΣΤΔ gets together for an academic conference, and in 2011 that conference was held in Pittsburgh, Pennsylvania. I love to travel, and so my chapter and I organized a panel on the mechanics of writing, and I also presented a couple papers (a research paper on Mary Shelley and a fiction work about my grandfather). I didn't know anything about hockey at the time, so when I noticed a game on the television at a local bar, it stuck with me. That evening, as we drove back to our hotel, we ran into traffic from that very game I had noticed on the TV. I took note of the jerseys and the joy, tucked it away as a curiosity, and didn't think about it again for years.

I don't play sports. To be honest, I don't even like board games or video games. I read a ton and watch a lot of television, but I've never really watched any sports except for high school volleyball and water polo (when my daughter played), the Super Bowl, and the NBA playoffs. I also lack the sort of citywide loyalty to the local home teams that so many of my neighbours exhibit. So, when hockey eventually came into my purview, I couldn't help but think of that special trip to Pittsburgh, and the black and yellow blur outside of the car window on that evening so long ago.

After grad school, I spent a lot of time writing and thinking about fandom—aca-fandom specifically, and the role of fans in the academic discourse around popular culture phenomena. In non-geek speak, I'm a fan of being a fan. And the most enduring fandom, the most accepted fandom in mainstream society, is sports. I decided I wanted to understand sports—that vestige of toxic masculinity and outdated physical expectations! I wanted to organically engage in a sport on my own terms, without the biases of those around me, and so I picked hockey, something I thought I could enjoy quietly. Ha! When I came into the hockey space, I realized that I could use my nerd skills to build something cool, not just for myself but for others who wanted to engage in sport but maybe never had an access point. So I took a chance, followed my gut, and built BGHC. *Might as well go all in, right?*

I didn't get to see the Pens play that night back in 2011, but the sight of their fans, their city, and their game sparked something in me that gave me pause and continues to inspire me. The Penguins team, the staff, the players, and the city of Pittsburgh aren't perfect, but they are committed to each other and the game of ice hockey. As a fan, I can respect that, and I certainly admire it. One of my favourite mistakes is when people think I'm from Pittsburgh. Nope! Born and raised in California, but I hope it's not too presumptuous of me to say that I'm a yinzer at heart.

LINCOLN AND SAROYA

When the 2020 Los Angeles Kings retro jersey commercial dropped on a Friday night in late 2019, I received no fewer than four text messages and a dozen tags on social media, all making sure that I had seen the little Black girl who lived in my city wearing the iconic '90s Kings jersey. The commercial featured Lincoln Brown, a twelve-year-old biracial Black girl and one of the best hockey players at her level in a city of hockey champions.

Lincoln's parents—Kelvin, an African American, and Rebecca, a Caucasian—moved to Los Angeles from Michigan and have been married for more than twenty years. In addition to Lincoln, and Kelvin's eldest daughter, Briana (25), the couple have two sons, Jaxon (19) and Reichen (17), who also play hockey. Lincoln, though, is the prodigy.

"She's been obsessed with hockey since she was born," her mother tells me over Zoom on a hot afternoon in May. The Browns are huddled together on the couch in their Central Los Angeles home while I sit in my office sixty miles away in Riverside, California. As the sun begins to set on a Friday evening, we settle into what will be the first of two conversations, and chat about Lincoln's love of hockey, navigating elite youth sports, and the distinct experience of being the parent of the only Black girl playing in a league of mostly white kids.

After the commercial aired, I invited Lincoln and the Browns to join me at a Black Girl Hockey Club event with the Los Angeles Kings in October 2019. The Brown family, myself, and twenty or so Black fans—including Blake Bolden, the first Black woman to ever play professional hockey—gathered together to see a hockey game: a simple, fun outing that remains one of the favourite activities of BGHC. That afternoon, I didn't get the chance to talk much with Lincoln, but I did make sure to snap a picture before she hopped onto the Zamboni between periods to represent our group for the entire arena to see.

Lincoln sits quietly most of the time, sometimes making faces at the answers her mother provides, sometimes chiming in with corrections or details that her parents don't know. When she talks about hockey, her face stretches into a grin, and she pokes her chin out with pride as she tells me about what she wants to do in the very near future.

"I want to go to prep school, but it's too expensive," she says.

"And too far!" Kelvin interrupts with a smile.

"It's all on the East Coast, too, so . . ." Rebecca offers as she looks at her husband and Lincoln. At this point, the choice has not been made, and there is a complicated path in front of Lincoln. In the past, she has played on both girls' and boys' teams, but as her skill level grows, she has to make some decisions.

I ask Rebecca and Kelvin how they figured out which team to place Lincoln on and how to deal with scouts at games, things like that. Rebecca laughs and shakes her head.

"In the beginning, we knew nothing. When my son started, I got gear donated to him and I had no idea his helmet was two sizes too big and his skates were a size three when he wore a kids' twelve. He was out there skating with a big helmet and some really big skates!

"We started off in roller hockey, then the L.A. Kings actually sponsored them and gave out free Kings tickets, so that's how we were introduced to ice hockey. We got to go see a Kings game and Lincoln [fell] in love with it from the beginning. We went to ice hockey, Junior Kings, and we had no idea about the levels. I just started at the bottom because I figured, you know, she's brand-new to it, we'll try out for the lowest B team, and of course she made it. I didn't know that you're supposed to start at the top and if you don't make that, you go down to the next level." Rebecca pauses. She takes a deep breath. "She did really well."

When the L.A. Lions program began in 2015, Lincoln was among the first players to join. She's grown up with the girls that she currently plays with. That's why switching to only playing with boys would be a big deal. The decision isn't to be made lightly, but for this family, none of the hockey ones are.

"I have no clue about how it's going to work or what we have to do. We're learning as we go, I guess. We have no guidance," Rebecca says.

"For the most part," Kelvin adds, "it's been going back and forth with other parents. Every now and then we'd get a coach who would mention something but never really go into detail on how to do it."

"Her coach claims to want to support her on whatever path she wants, but I also feel there's kind of a *we want to keep the girls here for our team*," Rebecca muses. "I know that a prep school actually approached our coach about [Lincoln] when they saw her play. He did give us the information—not all of it, I think. We just need to find a coach that fights for her and can give us . . ." She switches tactics. "Maybe he'll have had that same experience, going to prep school or . . ." Rebecca trails off. "I'm not really sure where to get that information from," she admits.

Absence of information is a common theme with BIPOC parents of hockey players. With few access points into hockey readily available in marginalized communities, the way hockey works—the prep schools, the clinics, the summer skates and conditioning programs, even finding the necessary equipment— can be a guessing game. Consistently, first-generation hockey parents have no clue how to navigate the complexities of youth hockey. Players put on about ten pieces of equipment before they skate onto the ice; goalies wear even more, and that gear is expensive, especially as kids grow and parents are forced to replace pieces each year. There are no Black professional head coaches in the NHL, no Black American women have ever played Olympic hockey, and only one Black American man has ever played in an Olympic hockey tournament—Jordan Greenway in 2018. As of 2024, neither USA Hockey nor Hockey Canada collects demographic information, so there is no way to tell how many BIPOC players there actually are in either of the national programs, but a look at the most recent World Championship rosters (and every single roster before that) speaks more than any chart or graph ever could.

Organizations like Black Girl Hockey Club, the Columbus Ice Hockey Club, and Hockey Players of Color (HPOC) Movement combat this gatekeeping by working together to provide information to parents and skaters that will help them continue in hockey as long as they like. For Lincoln, a couple of well-timed conversations have me offering up the contact information of a colleague and co-conspirator who is knowledgeable about prep schools because his sons attend. Even though I'm interviewing the Browns for reasons outside of my work with Black Girl Hockey Club, I can't help but puzzle a few pieces together and do my best to unite Black folks breaking barriers in hockey. It's an important and underrated part of my work—connecting Black folks to whatever resources BGHC has available. I don't know how to do everything, but I do know how to connect dots.

I put the Browns in touch with Michael Watson, long-time leader with the Columbus Ice Hockey Club board of directors, Black hockey dad, and member of the Black Girl Hockey Club advocacy campaign committee. "Coach Mike," as his players and friends call him, is an African American man who fell in love with the game of hockey as a parent of a precocious three-year-old. His son, Spencer, enrolled at Culver Military Academy to play high school hockey, and now plays for Dartmouth College. At first, though, Mike had no idea how to navigate the system.

"Because of how I grew up," he starts, "we didn't have a lot of money, so you figured out how to be creative to progress your skills. I just got creative in helping [Spencer] learn how to skate and feed his passion. Early on, I'm not going to lie, I had to learn, and that's where Columbus Ice Hockey Club came in.

"One of the local papers did [an article on] the current director of Columbus Ice Hockey Club, John Haferman.

What really resonated with me was . . . the population that they serve. I'm in an interracial relationship, so Spencer's mother is white, I'm African American. I've always looked for opportunities for Spence to see people who look like his father doing the things that he is interested in. This is an opportunity to be around other African American kids, women, people you normally wouldn't see skating, skating! Up until then, the only two Black people in the rink would be me and Spence. Spence is very fair-skinned, so I would be standing on the boards or sitting in the stands and the other team had a Black kid who was my complexion, and parents would be like, 'So, how long's your son been playing hockey?' Pointing at a kid that's not my son."

After fifteen years working in the Columbus hockey community, Coach Mike continues to build a pipeline to ice hockey for Black and marginalized communities. He understands how important certain opportunities are for up-and-coming hockey players, as well as how difficult it is for first-generation hockey parents to access that information—particularly when it comes to topics such as the connection between hockey-focused boarding schools and college or professional scouting. His son attended an elite boarding school as one of the only Black kids on the hockey team. Together, the Watson family put time into researching scholarship opportunities, team dynamics, coaching staff, race relations on campus, academic integrity, and future prospects before settling on what they agreed was the best option for Spencer.

"People talk about money. That's one of three pillars you have to break right in order to be successful in this game. One is money, two is time, and three is access," he states with the air of someone who has listed these things before. "We'll dig into what I mean by access," Mike promises before I can ask him to explain. "Having access to the appropriate information, network, training, and competitive environment in order to be successful."

The definition is simple and clear. Access for Black hockey parents and other first-generation hockey parents of marginalized folks can prove difficult without guidance, and is near impossible when parents lack the money and time. So many Black parents decide that hockey just isn't worth it. The financial commitment—in addition to the long hours of practice, driving to games, tournament weekends, and more—plus the lack of representation on and off the ice, and the troubling consistency of racism in youth hockey across North America, perpetuate a low interest in the sport among Black communities. For those Black players and fans who do decide to take up the game in spite of the gatekeeping, there hasn't been a successful effort by professional hockey to engage them as a demographic or really even acknowledge their presence in the game. The National Hockey League only began publicly acknowledging Black History Month in 2019. As of 2023, Hockey Canada has a murky anti-discrimination policy aimed at "any player or team official who engages in taunts, insults, or intimidation based on discriminatory grounds," which sounds like a loose standard, potentially subject to the whims of game-day referees. The lack of cohesion and care toward marginalized communities is clearly delineated by the lack of access for these same communities.

For Lincoln and the Browns, the burgeoning community being built by and for marginalized folks in hockey brings an opportunity to gain access to, as Coach Mike puts it, "the appropriate information, network, training, and competitive environment" to succeed. Those factors, while so simple, aren't always easy to come by. Without mentors in the industry, first-generation hockey families of colour do not possess the tools or resources that many of their non-BIPOC peers acquire through networking and social connections.

Only a few months after I introduce the Browns to Coach Mike, I get a text from him that simply says, "Lincoln got into Culver!" With Coach Mike advocating, guiding, and offering resources, they were able to find a pathway for Lincoln to realize her dream of attending a prestigious hockey boarding school. That summer, BGHC organizes two webinars offering guidance from Lisa Marshall, the girls' varsity head hockey coach and admissions counsellor at Berkshire School; Nikki Chambers, Dean of Diversity, Equity, Inclusion, and Belonging at the Williston Northampton School; Mike Watson; and Rebecca Warner, Lincoln's mom. We sit down for a couple of one-hour sessions on a late September evening, after East Coast and West Coast hockey practices are finished, and go over the things that we think Black kids need to know about hockey boarding schools and academies. What is the environment like for someone who is one of the only Black hockey players on campus (if not the only one)? How do students gain access to scholarships and grants? What are the practical steps to take in order to have a successful admissions interview?

It is a powerful lesson that there are people who recognize the disparities faced by Black folks in hockey and are working to shift that narrative to benefit more marginalized folks within the community. By taking the time to gather experts, and offering these webinars on hockey schools for Black kids that now live on the BGHC YouTube channel, BGHC has created a practical, high-impact, and outside-the-box way of ensuring access to hockey for all.

Unlike Lincoln, Saroya Tinker did not have a hockey support system that included Black folks, so she forged her own path to success. Some might know Saroya as the professional Black hockey player who went up against Barstool Sports and their "Stoolies" during the 2021 NWHL playoffs, when she tweeted an unequivocal renouncement of the media company for its racist and misogynistic history and was viciously trolled on social media as a result. The Barstool incident introduced Saroya, Black Girl Hockey Club, and allies to folks on the "other side" of the issues of inclusion and equity. Sports media companies like ESPN and Sportsnet picked up the story and brought attention to Saroya's anti-racism work in hockey. But the professional hockey player and Black Girl Hockey Club volunteer hadn't found her voice as an unapologetic Black girl overnight.

Saroya is biracial, with thick gorgeous dark hair and a smile that lights up her face. Born and raised in Oshawa, Ontario, she started skating at two years old and began competitive gymnastics before joining a local boys' house league at six and falling in love with the game of hockey. When she wanted to get serious about the sport, Saroya tried out for the Oshawa Lady Generals and started playing competitively with other girls at the age of ten.

"When I played for the Lady Generals there was one other [Black] girl on my team, she was lighter than me but she was mixed. I just played with her for one year but I feel like, at that point, it wasn't really acknowledged that we were different, it was just that we were women playing hockey. I think there were a few mixed boys that I played against but weren't on my team. I've played with Asian players, in terms of BIPOC community, but never anybody who was any darker than me." Saroya shakes her head, a sad smile on her lips. "Which is weird to think about."

"Growing up in Oshawa—a very white town—I don't think I ever had a Black girlfriend in Oshawa. That . . . like . . . no." She stumbles over her words. "No name comes to mind, which is kinda weird *and* annoying. I was being made fun of by the other girls at school. I didn't have another Black role model to look up to. My mom's white. My mom doesn't necessarily understand that. As much as she wants to and as much as she tries, I know that she never will."

Excelling as a player on the Yale University team and being drafted by the PHF's Metropolitan Riveters in 2020 did not help Saroya relate to her mostly white teammates, who seemed to live in a bubble of privilege and ignorance. The microaggressions and the covert sexism and racism that Saroya had felt her entire hockey career came to a head while she was playing in the 2021 women's hockey (WoHo) playoffs with the Riveters. A rookie in just her third week with the team, Saroya headed into the playoff space created during the COVID-19 pandemic, which WoHo fans affectionately called the "bubble." She received a swag bag from the National Women's Hockey League that included a T-shirt from Barstool Sports, the American digital media company founded by Dave Portnoy in 2003 that produces content on sports and pop culture.

In all honesty, I had no desire to write about this company and get on the Stoolie radar, but here we are, dear reader. If you have remained blissfully unaware until now, I hate to break it to you, but Barstool Sports is known for being unapologetic in their discriminatory language and treatment of marginalized folks, with a fanbase—"Stoolies"—that attacks anyone who dares speak out against the company ethos. Unfortunately, many professional hockey players support Barstool in spite of their reputation among marginalized communities, including some of the players on the 2021 Metropolitan Riveters. Prior to the launch of the bubble, Barstool CEO girlboss Erika Nardini expressed interest in buying a stake in the NWHL on her podcast when two of Saroya's teammates at the time joined the show to hype the beginning of the season for Barstool's audience. The backlash from WoHo fans against Barstool was swift but mild compared to what came next. In retaliation, Nardini posted a video to her Twitter account identifying her biggest naysayers by name, sparking a slew of vitriol and hate from Stoolies mainly against women hockey fans. Rather than apologizing for the sexist, misogynistic, and racist content created by the media company, Portnoy, Nardini, and Barstool railed against "cancel culture" and public "pressure for conformity," encouraging similar attacks on anyone who opposed their views.

When Saroya brought up the topic of Barstool to then NWHL Players' Association director Anya Packer, the league assured Saroya that the Barstool brand was not compatible with professional women's hockey. The swag disappeared, but Saroya still wanted to use her platform to assure marginalized WoHo fans that Barstool values had no place in the professional league, and so she tweeted out her displeasure, not really knowing what and *who* she was going up against: "WE, as a league do not want support from ANY openly racist platform. Point blank, PERIOD. If you, as the CEO cannot recognize that your platform promotes that of white supremacy & only further divides the athletic community, perhaps we need [to] have a conversation. Pls keep your money."

The tweet garnered violent, rude, and over-the-top trolling from Stoolies. "I didn't expect all that just because I mean, I don't even engage with Barstool," Saroya tells me. "I know what it is, but at the same time, I don't want anything to do with it. So, I didn't know about the Stoolie attack that I was about to receive. My phone just started blowing up.

"I don't think what I said was wrong. I fully stand behind what I said. Again, if [Erika Nardini] wanted to have a conversation with me, I'm here for it. Not my job, but I'm here for it. And, yeah, everything just kind of blew up from there. I talked to the NWHL commissioner, and she let me know that she was absolutely disgusted by the video, and really disappointed in the players that decided to participate in the podcast and let me know that the league wasn't supporting it, and that they stood by me.

"And obviously, I'm not here to speak on behalf of my league. But that was how I felt as a player. And that's exactly how I would have felt if we did accept their sponsorship. So that's why I chose to say something.

"I didn't know how to necessarily handle it, especially as a rookie on the team who'd been there for three weeks. Like no one—no one really knows me other than what they see on social. Yeah. But the extent of what I was going through . . ." She trails off and then starts again. "Obviously, on social, I was positive and everything. I was crying in my room, I was receiving death threats, as a twenty-three-year-old, and then, the comments. People were commenting about Yale, people commenting about my privilege and things like that. And yes, it's easy to ignore the negative stuff. But obviously, there's a few comments here and there that get to me.

"I could hear this girl," Saroya says. "I don't know who it was in the hotel room next to me. But she was on the phone with her parents and they said, 'Oh, that stupid girl didn't have to say anything about Barstool, that really could have helped you.' And I was just so mad at that point. I screamed, 'I can fucking hear you!' at the wall. I was like, *Oh my god.* I was really trying to hold my composure and grace through it all, which I did. But there were definitely some not-so-nice things said and things like that. It was just a different thing that I've never experienced. I didn't expect it. And I also, I honestly don't think I expected my teammates to be in support. I'm not used to them supporting me in that sense or understanding. So it was kinda like, *Well, I understand why you don't understand. But at the same time, it's how I feel, and I don't care how you feel.*"

As she continues to build her own community in hockey, Saroya holds the unique perspective of a professional Black ice hockey player, and can speak to the specific obstacles our younger BGHC skaters face now—and in the future, if they decide to pursue a similar path. After working closely with Black Girl Hockey Club's scholarship program for a full season, Saroya decided she wanted to take the work off of Zoom and into the streets of Toronto, where, in 2021, she was traded to play for the Toronto Six. Saroya has high hopes for Black girls in hockey, and it shows in our co-founding of Black Girl

Hockey Club Canada in 2022—an iteration of BGHC based out of Toronto, with Saroya at the helm as executive director and me on the board. This charity organization acts as a network for young Black girl hockey players, taking our online work directly into the hockey community of Toronto.

"The more girls I get into my mentorship program, the more I realize . . . there's so much potential for us to just . . . take over," Saroya says. Over the course of two separate interviews at the end of 2021, Saroya and I spent our time talking about a slew of topics. At that point, BGHC Canada was just an idea, not even fully realized yet, but the seeds were sown in order to grow something amazing out of the fertile ground BGHC had already laid across the United States. As I write this at the end of 2023, BGHC Canada has officially operated for a full year, secured partnerships and funding from large Canadian donors, and hosted the first of hopefully many hockey camps with Black coaches and players from all over North America. The impact of Black women in hockey keeps growing.

"I really want to make sure we have a network to continue to be able to bring Black women into hockey," Saroya tells me. "Because for myself, I didn't know Kim Davis. I knew Sarah Nurse, but I never would have reached out to her during my career. I want Black girls to be able to feel like they can do that and feel like they have a support system, because I felt like I had no one to talk to. And I think that's why I do what I do. I see Black Girl Hockey Club doing that for them."

"I've opened [my mailing list] up to all BIPOC women in sport, but at the same time I would say there's probably four or five that just, like, enjoy coming to our Zoom workouts and enjoy my posts and things like that. I think my youngest right now is nine, and the oldest I have is like twenty-seven. There's also girls that are reporters or are involved in the hockey community in another sense that want to join. I think that's important for not only my girls that are being recruited, but for the ones that just need a community and people to talk to.

"I feel like my mom finding Black Girl Hockey Club— 'cause my mom's the one that found you guys and everything—is probably the reason I'm still playing, because I was done with it. That's definitely one of the biggest reasons why I still play; because I actually found a community."

This isn't the only time Saroya has spoken publicly about her love/hate relationship with ice hockey. In February 2021, she wrote an article for the *Players' Tribune* about the challenges she has faced in the game and how the BGHC community helped her find her place. In November 2023, Saroya retired from playing and, in its inaugural season, began working as the Manager of DEI Initiatives and Community Engagement with the PWHL, while offering commentary behind the broadcast desk as a PWHL analyst for CBC Sports. Within these roles, as well as in her mentorships and work with BGHC, Saroya uses her own experiences in the sport to guide how she affects a culture change in ice hockey.

It was her father who introduced her to hockey, but Saroya didn't initially recognize the colour of their skin as an othering factor until she started examining the way her father was treated at the rink. Microaggressions are incredibly difficult to pinpoint because the bar is always moving, but Saroya began to notice that she was not being judged on skill alone.

"I just knew it was a game that my dad loved . . . but I didn't realize what my dad was going through. My parents never have been hockey parents. You get the politics and . . . my parents are not like that at all, so they always kind of stood off by themselves. Later on, I realized my mom stood off by herself because she didn't like the way people treated my dad at the arena. Whether it was just the casual 'Yeah, I'll talk to you here but when I'm in a big group of white men talking about our kids playing you're the person I don't know anymore' toward my dad, I think that really bothered my mom."

I met the Tinker family via email back when I was planning Black Girl Hockey Club's first-ever trip to see the Pittsburgh Penguins play at their home arena. In April 2019, I'd connected with two of the very few Black women executives working in professional hockey: Tracey McCants Lewis, Deputy General Counsel and Director of Human Resources, and Delvina Morrow, Director of Strategic and Community Engagement for the Pittsburgh Penguins at the time. We quickly recognized our shared values in terms of community-building and equity in hockey spaces, and we worked together to create a very special event to kick off Black History Month 2020 in Pittsburgh. Tracey and Delvina demonstrate what intentionality and authentic engagement with the Black hockey community can accomplish. They even got the mayor of Pittsburgh, Bill Peduto, to declare January 31 "Black Hockey History Day" in the Steel City, but the most outstanding thing to me is that the team didn't do this silently. They promoted the event just like they would any other theme night. They added a special ticket link to their website, created graphics, and dropped PR announcements, ensuring that information about the event was widespread and easily accessible to local Black hockey fans. The night of the game— aptly nicknamed "the Battle of Pennsylvania," highlighting the rivalry between the Philadelphia Flyers and the Pittsburgh Penguins—more than 500 tickets were sold through the Black Hockey History promotional link on the Penguins website.

Mandy and Harvel Tinker, Saroya's parents, came across this event through the BGHC newsletter, and Mandy emailed me to RSVP for five guests—including Saroya, who was then a senior at Yale University. Mandy followed up her email with a note identifying that she was white and she wanted to bring along her Black husband and their biracial children, Saroya, Malachi, and Dondre. What I didn't realize at the time was that the entire family would be taking a 300-mile-long road trip from Oshawa to Pittsburgh in order to celebrate Black hockey excellence with Black Girl Hockey Club. The Tinkers joined me and forty-five other BGHC attendees at PPG Paints Arena bright and early on Friday morning for a tour and breakfast, and then again on Saturday at the August Wilson centre for the *Soul on Ice* screening about (male) Black hockey players. After the film, and with Kim Davis in attendance for support, BGHC and the Penguins hosted a panel with director Kwame Mason, NHI.com writer and Black hockey historian Bill Douglas, myself, and local Pittsburgh hockey leaders, to discuss youth hockey in the city and what could be done to be more inclusive toward Black residents. What struck me about the family attending the event wasn't the fact that they drove over 300 miles to hang out with other Black hockey fans, but the email that Mandy sent to me a few days after the event detailing some of her fears and struggles as the white mother of a Black girl hockey player. Mandy let me know that she could not comprehend her daughter's experiences, and she thanked me for providing a space where players and fans like her kids could thrive. The fact that Mandy recognized the gap that Saroya herself would later articulate, and worked with all her motherly might to find a way to fill it, goes to show her commitment to creating safe hockey spaces for her daughter and others who look like her.

Unfortunately, I didn't get to meet Saroya in Pittsburgh. She backed out at the last minute to attend a hockey tournament with her team at Yale. But after the COVID-19 shutdown that spring, I was asked by the National Women's Hockey League (later renamed the Premier Hockey Federation) to announce her as the Metropolitan Riveters' draft pick on the league's Twitch stream. I pre-recorded the message to Saroya, and afterwards I reached out to invite her to chat with me on the first official BGHC Instagram Live stream, in early June 2020. We talked hockey, community, and the Black Lives Matter movement, and about the need for Black leaders for up-and-coming Black players. Saroya subsequently joined our scholarship committee and offered to mentor BGHC scholarship awardees, kicking off the Saroya Strong Mentorship Program and cementing her commitment to Black Girl Hockey Club's mission and values. A few months later, in the midst of the Barstool controversy, Saroya would use her platform to raise more than $30,000, which we used as seed money to eventually launch BGHC Canada. When Lincoln Brown received her $1,000 scholarship from Black Girl Hockey Club, I directed her to Saroya's program, and Lincoln has been able to chat with other Black girl hockey players, work out with her friends on Zoom, and have direct access not only to Saroya but to a network of Black women involved in hockey. It's a full-circle effort to encourage and engage Black girls in hockey that folks like Mike Watson, Saroya Tinker, and I take very seriously.

If you take a look at the comment section of the YouTube video for Lincoln's Los Angeles Kings jersey reveal, you will see hints of the vitriol aimed at Black women in sports—but the hockey version of this misogynoir, aimed at a twelve-year old, is especially disturbing. Lincoln, though, is discovering that she has a support system surrounding her that will shield, fight, and work with her as long as she wants to play hockey—which, according to Lincoln, will be quite a long time. And she hasn't experienced much first-hand bigotry, which is a blessing.

Lincoln decided to play exclusively on the boys' team after our first interview. During her first tournament with the new team, Lincoln played defence, even though that isn't her natural position, and she was excited to tell me about the goal she scored during one of their games.

Her mom, though, told me something else about the experience. "Last weekend, at our tournament in St. Louis, we played five games and on each team that we played there was at least one player of colour, which was really great to see. This is usually not the case. In one of the games, however, we were told that Lincoln's teammate was checked into the boards and the other team's player said something like 'Stay down, Black boy.' After the game, Lincoln told us, 'The other team was racist to Myles.'

"This is the first time something like this has come so close and into the bubble for her. I don't know all of the details or what was said exactly, but I do know the issue was reported, we were all angry and disappointed, our whole team was supportive, and Myles and his family would like to come to the next BGHC event with Lincoln."

This type of casual racism on the ice, with little to no discipline at the moment of the attack, can be found at all levels of hockey, but is especially prevalent in youth hockey. So far, Lincoln has been sheltered from racism and sexism in sport, but her decision to play boys' hockey has marked a shift in her commitment to the sport. Along with the higher level of competitiveness that comes with playing on the boys' team there's a higher chance that race, gender, sexuality, ability, and other intersections will separate players like Lincoln and Myles from the traditional hockey market. Without official policies, training, and accountability structures, intersectional identities will continue to be used as weapons, turned against anyone different or anyone who dares speak against the hegemony of hockey culture. This is why building a network of BIPOC and other marginalized folks in hockey is so revolutionary, and why it's so important that Myles and his people know more about BGHC and the support system that surrounds them.

The thing is, the players, executives, and fans who stick around hockey in spite of all the bad stuff are not necessarily stronger than those who leave the game. Trauma is tiring. So many racialized players and fans walk away from hockey, not wanting to spend their money or time on a sport that has more than its fair share of abuse allegations and racist incidents. There is financial gatekeeping that comes in the shape of tournament fees and equipment costs, and the task of navigating the intricate web that is scouting, hockey schools and academies, and college or junior hockey. The lack of access points has made hockey a hill that many Black folks just don't care to try to climb. But there are some in the hockey space who hope that the game we love will be better, if not for us directly then for those who come after. Within this space, self-care, communication, and grace are given and taken freely. These values permeate the work of Coach Mike, Saroya Tinker, and every member and volunteer in the Black Girl Hockey Club network. Saroya Tinker and Lincoln Brown are coming to understand that their presence on the ice is resistance; their mentorship relationship subversive; the community they are a part of revolutionary.

HOCKEY MAMAS

There is no blueprint for becoming a hockey mom. Some have been around the sport their entire lives and have passed a familial love of the game to their children. Some hockey moms have the sport introduced to them by their kids, who drag Mom to the rink every Saturday morning until it starts to feel a lot like home. Others marry into the game, and watch as their partners inundate their kids with a hockey love so pronounced that Mom ends up falling for the sport too. A few engage with the game begrudgingly, but none can get away with doing the bare minimum—not in hockey. It is a sport that preaches teamwork, togetherness, equality on the ice. Parents of players must be involved as much as they can, and as kids get older, better at the game, and even move toward the goal of collegiate or professional sports, being a hockey mom can become a full-time job.

For those who are mothers of Black children who play hockey, diversity and equity issues in the game make it so that the sport isn't as simple as hockey culture would like us to pretend. The rinkside experience can be intimidating for

Black mothers, as well as non-Black moms of Black children. Of course, Black parents and non-Black parents of Black children face discrimination in hockey differently. Non-Black parents may observe, internalize, and react to anti-Black racism, while Black parents can become the targets of harassment and microaggressions themselves. There are arenas that are actually *frightening* to visit; teams that are more volatile than others; coaches and parents who disregard discrimination issues from their players because their team *wins games*; hockey governing bodies that do not put consistent policies in place to keep kids safe from abuse and turn a blind eye when bad things happen. While there are many hockey organizations that claim to be committed to eradicating discrimination as well as addressing the tangible needs of marginalized players through infrastructure and policy development, the stats tell a different tale. Black hockey players are few and far between at all levels of hockey, which means that equitable communities must be built with intentionality. Parents of Black children will seek these spaces out, but first they must exist.

Currently, there are a growing number of grassroots organizations that focus on diversifying hockey and supporting marginalized players and their families. RGV Roller, HPOC Movement, Minnesota Unbounded, Saroya Strong, Columbus Ice Hockey Club, OWN Aces Sports Group, Hockey Equality, Fort Dupont Cannons, Ice Hockey in Harlem, Hockey 4 Youth, APNA Hockey, and Ball Hockey Boot Camp are all programs that work toward making hockey a more welcoming space for Black and brown kids. These are groups that centre the experiences and needs of BIPOC hockey players and families in order to make the sport more equitable for everyone involved. For these hockey organizations, values such as logistical and financial accessibility as well as representation for the most marginalized among us are the keys to building a successful and sustainable hockey community within marginalized spaces. Most, if not all, of the programs listed above were started or are currently run by BIPOC hockey fans, players, and parents. These are folks stepping up to create access to hockey within their own communities because traditional hockey institutions continue to fail marginalized folks.

Lisa Ramos, mother of Ayodele Adeniye, found her hockey community at the Columbus Ice Hockey Club (CIHC) after Ayo discovered the sport at the age of four. During the 2021–22 season, Ayo started playing NCAA Division III hockey at Adrian College in Michigan, a dream almost twenty years in the making, and he has high hopes of making it to the Big Show. Ayodele is committed to hockey, and because of that, so is his mother. As a parent of one of the few Black college athletes to play NCAA hockey, Lisa takes being a hockey mom seriously. Even though Ayo moved on from Columbus to go to school and play hockey in Ontario with the Carleton Place Canadians for two seasons, from the ages of nineteen to twenty-one, he and his mother continue to support the community that uplifted their family at a time when they needed it the most. Not only did Lisa make sure that Ayo played and practised with coaches who cared, she also sat on the board of directors for the Columbus Ice Hockey Club as treasurer during those early years. Still, while the city of Columbus is itself diverse, the local hockey scene is not. Community leaders such as John Haferman, Jeff Christian, Mike Watson, and Lisa Ramos of the CIHC work so that the Black kids who want to play can.

This means offering tangible services such as rides, mentorships, and equipment, while meeting the kids where they are in order to foster a love of hockey in a safe and welcoming environment. Though, according to Lisa, what was once a program for predominantly Black and brown kids has turned into a haven for middle-class, non-minority (read: white) families from the suburbs who are looking to save money on fees.

"When we first started, there were a lot more Black kids there and a lot more older Black kids. As [CIHC has] gone through the years, they don't have as many minorities as they used to have. Part of that is because it's a city Parks and Rec [club]. A lot of suburbanites find out that it's cheap and they'll come over and get in. I mean, the team is so much cheaper, because we try to make sure that it's affordable. But you get a lot of suburbanites that are running over." Lisa pauses, noting another point in the narrative that we haven't discussed yet—the lack of physical accessibility to suburban hockey rinks for non-white kids living in urban areas.

"The other thing is, it still is very difficult to get, you know, African American kids interested in hockey. And the best way that John [Haferman] and those guys still continue to do that is through floor hockey. Once they play floor hockey, they enjoy it. Unlike baseball or basketball, you can't just jump on the ice and play hockey, you have to learn how to skate first. And that is costly and difficult.

"They're trying to get a rink in the urban areas, right? Like, I don't want to say 'the hood,' but it will be in an urban area. That would change demographics for hockey in Columbus because the kids can't actually get to the rink right now. Where the ice rink is, the only way that they can get there is if John picks them up, or one of the centres picks them up and takes them out there because [the rinks] are all in suburban areas."

Lisa shakes her head. Her frustration is clear. While Lisa and Ayo were lucky enough to find leadership committed to authentic engagement with Black families to develop youth hockey in Columbus, not everyone has the same opportunities. Without the support of CIHC, Ayodele might not be playing NCAA hockey right now. The community at CIHC offers players much more than just a place on the roster; there is an understanding between coaches, board members, and parents that the kids come first. Lisa acknowledges that part of the value of creating fellowship with folks that she shares a cultural background with is that there is no need to justify or explain the space that she and her family take up in hockey. The Columbus Ice Hockey Club and the leadership there are committed to inclusion. There is Black leadership that focuses on the tangible needs of Black families, and they work together with Black parents to create a space where players like Ayodele can not only succeed, but feel safe and compelled to contribute and make the experience of playing hockey while Black a more positive one for the kids who come after. It isn't just the parents who take up the cause of inclusion in hockey.

"The players themselves are making a change. They're linking up and they're supporting each other. They're not waiting for support from the outside. Social media is allowing them to do that. They're seeking each other out. That's one of the reasons why I think they're finding strength to lift each other up, which, when they were younger, they didn't have.

"You don't have to be a big player to come back and help these younger kids because the numbers are small. Those kids still need support, and they still need mentoring and to know how to navigate through those waters. I think what has been a major difference is the people that have navigated through that are reaching back and talking to the younger ones."

Creating and sustaining meaningful relationships between Black hockey players, parents, executives, and fans is instrumental to the growth of the game in Black communities. For Lisa, one of those connections came when she met Coach Mike Watson. Together, they helped grow the CIHC program not only for their own children, but for the communities around them, by improving the cultural competence within the organization, its players, and staff.

In practical terms, this means addressing not just the immediate negative repercussions of discriminatory acts, but following through with coaches and players to address micro-aggressions so that they don't happen again. This also means recruiting volunteers and staff members who represent the served communities, and vetting partnerships, administrators, and board members on a regular basis to ensure that they remain committed to developing effective and appropriate cognitive, affective, and behavioural skills in order to communicate with people of all cultures and identities. It means getting involved with the team and staff development, and stepping up for the parents who do not have the means or the privilege to take time off work to do all these things. It means going into marginalized communities to meet folks where they are. Black and brown communities do not often have ready access to ice or hockey equipment, so ball or street hockey is a more practical way to get these kids excited about the sport. Meanwhile, a mixed-abilities tournament that includes sled hockey and/or blind hockey could open up opportunities on the ice for a lot of players and give disabled fans something to get excited about.

Non-Black folks must also speak up for Black parents and players when they are not in the room! The work of diversifying hockey and making it equitable for all should not fall on the shoulders of marginalized folks. In order for these organizations and the values they uphold to root themselves in hockey, we must all pick up the slack to protect marginalized communities both on and off the ice.

In the last few years, there has been an uptick of Black-run hockey organizations, and I'm proud to know that Black Girl Hockey Club is part of a growing network of equitable spaces in hockey. After talking to Rebecca Warner and Kelvin Brown, parents of two-time BGHC scholarship awardee Lincoln Brown, I realized that hockey prep schools are one of the options that parents of first-generation hockey players don't always know how to explore. And so in September 2022, the BGHC volunteer team held a series of webinars for Black hockey players interested in the hockey prep school admission process. In order for the event to be a success, we had to make sure to address the access issues that marginalized families experience when engaging in youth hockey, particularly in the specialized academic setting of prep schools. We wanted to cover not only the financial costs but also the social and cultural shifts that Black students end up having to make in these spaces.

Along with other Black- and brown-run organizations, we are helping to pave a path for Black women in this sport and creating room for those who come after us. With that in mind, the BGHC goal is to be a clearing house of information for all parents of all Black hockey players, especially Black girls. So many parents and players want to move forward with the sport, but don't know how to enrol their kids in skills development, how to navigate national youth hockey programs, or even what equipment to buy and where. These are just a few of the practical issues we try to tackle with the volunteers, parents, and members of BGHC, because the national organizations do not consistently offer these types of access points to Black hockey players and their families.

This is something I talked about with Joel Ward, assistant coach of the Vegas Golden Knights, who acknowledged why an organization like BGHC could have been meaningful for his own mother, Cecilia, while he was growing up.

Joel Ward is an Afro-Caribbean Canadian who played professional hockey for the Minnesota Wild, Nashville Predators, Washington Capitals, and San Jose Sharks. He officially retired from playing in 2020, and in the same year became a founding member of the Hockey Diversity Alliance, a first-of-its-kind organization run by professional BIPOC players with a mission to "eradicate systemic racism and intolerance in hockey." My first conversation with Joel takes place at the 2020 Black Girl Hockey Club Juneteenth digital panel event, during which myself, Joel, Ayo Adeniye, Blake Bolden, and Saroya Tinker discuss our experiences in hockey with hosts Erica Ayala and Sydney Augustine. Joel mentions that his mother would have appreciated BGHC and the work that we do because she herself had a rough time watching her son play hockey as he was coming up in the 1990s and the early 2000s. As he talks, Joel becomes emotional talking about the impact his mother has had on his hockey career.

"Yeah, so my mother, she is a humongous hockey fan," he begins. "A humongous Maple Leafs fan, you know? We had VHS tapes of my mother screaming in the background when my brothers were scoring. I wish we still had that VHS because you can hear there's a couple of them where Mom was just screaming in the background and to see her . . ." He laughs at the memory, trailing off before he gets serious. "Yeah, no, but her experience was mixed. You know, her love for the game. Sometimes you would see Mom in the corner sitting in the stands and she's not as included with the other folks and the other parents. But my mother knew the game, probably more than half the people *at* the game, you know?

"My mother worked two jobs. She was a registered nurse, but found a way to always provide. If I needed new hockey skates, Mom did not even flinch. She just somehow found a way. I'm like, man, my mother, the love that she had for us when it came . . . *especially* when it came to hockey, was through the roof. You know, my mother sacrificed—working shifts just so I could get to practice. I remember sleeping at the hospital because my mother had to work the night shift. So, after the game, she dragged me over, found a bed in the hospital and then took me home."

Joel's story is one that stays with me. I keep coming back to the complicated relationship that his mother had with hockey—as a fan, as a hockey mom, and as a Black woman. Joel's support for BGHC comes from a deep love for his mother and a recognition of the work that she did to get him to where he is now. On February 23, 2020, Joel Ward wore a Black Girl Hockey Club hoodie to drop the puck for the nationally televised Black History Month NHL rivalry game between the Pittsburgh Penguins and the Washington Capitals. With Sidney Crosby on one side and Alexander Ovechkin on the other, he sported a hoodie with our original logo on it in red (for the Caps). My Black hockey community worked hard to get that hoodie in Joel's hands by game day, and the national coverage brought many new eyes to the work that BGHC does in the hockey community.

When I ask Joel why he decided to support Black Girl Hockey Club in such a public way, the response, of course, involves his mom. "I talked to Bill [Douglas] a little bit, and being in DC, it just made me want to represent Black History Month. You know, my mother was . . . man . . ." He stops and shakes his head, getting emotional. "She [had to be] so powerful for me to get a chance to play hockey. And knowing what you're doing with your organization and group, it was only fitting for me to represent you guys. It just brings it back home. DC, too, is very special to my heart. I was there for many years in Chocolate City and it was a lot of fun. My mother loved it. You know, for me, I wanted to just represent an organization that represented me, and Black Girl Hockey Club was something that I could a hundred, a thousand per cent relate to. There was no other option; I had to. For me it is to kind of just give back as well. And to give back to you guys. What you guys are doing is very special to me. It's amazing to see what you guys are doing, so it was an honour to put the sweater on, drop the puck, and to give back. It was really cool."

The community that builds from supporting Black women in hockey is evident, but there is something special about the way Black folks lift one another up, particularly in white spaces. The support, the encouragement, and the way we spend our money and our time giving back to one another is unmatched! Some of my favourite in-arena moments include interactions with Black staff and fans who learn about BGHC for the first time from an intermission interview broadcast over the Jumbotron, and then we meet in the elevator or on the concourse, where they heap loads of love onto me and my organization. Oftentimes, Black folks are surprised, delighted, and ready to tell their friends about us, because of the unique space that BGHC provides for Black women in hockey. The confidence that Black folks give each other invigorates and energizes the work. So far, mainstream hockey culture has not provided these types of supportive spaces for Black women, and so we create them and vitalize them ourselves. At that 2020 Black History Month game in DC, Joel not only gave Black Girl Hockey Club encouragement, he then felt it himself just travelling through the arena after puck drop.

"Through the concourse, people were coming up to me and asking me questions, and ushers, again, that I've known over the course of the years were, you know, everybody was excited about it. I didn't know the impact; I just wanted to represent and to kind of give a shout-out so to speak, and to say thank you. And to let people know that this is an organization to support and so I'm glad that it helped out."

I get a kick out of informing Joel of the reactions that Black fans had when he wore his BGHC hoodie on national television, and that the BGHC merchandise store had an influx of visitors who supported the organization by purchasing items or giving cash donations. Black hockey players and fans who had never heard of BGHC had the chance not only to learn about the work that we do, but also to connect with us and become part of the BGHC family. After that day, it seemed like the larger hockey organizations and media companies began to take our work more seriously. I mean, we made it onto Joel Ward's back on live television! There should be no doubt about the impact that Black Girl Hockey Club is having and will continue to have on hockey culture if we can garner the full support of Black hockey communities. For me, that starts with the hockey mamas and how they feel watching their Black kids play a predominantly white sport.

Joel talks about how he was hyperaware of racial issues when he began playing hockey as a teenager in the late 1990s in the Ontario Hockey League (OHL), starting with his first billeting experience. "I was all of a sudden moved into an all-white family in Owen Sound. I remember just saying, 'Hey, I don't think I can do this' to my brother and my mom. And my family was like, 'You know what, you came this far, you've got to stick it out. You can always come home.'

"White folks would see me as a Black guy playing hockey, and it really had an effect on me. I moved to Owen Sound—a predominantly white town—to play hockey, and I realized that it was my duty to give back to the kids, especially the Black kids. I tried to interact with everybody. I had Black ushers at games tell me they loved coming to the games, because I was on the team. It was just so powerful knowing that I was playing the game for not just myself and my team, but for people of colour from all different backgrounds and neighbourhoods. I wanted to carry that weight, because people were proud of it and wanted to come to the game to see me play. I knew from a pretty early age that it was my responsibility to just spread the good word."

Even though his career started more than twenty years ago, Joel's experiences are so similar to the stories I continue to hear from hockey moms now. The lack of information, the nepotism, the microaggressions, and the lack of concern for the needs of Black players haven't changed much in the two and a half decades since he began his hockey career. It is also so important to acknowledge how much representation matters—to players, parents, and fans. For folks like the ushers in Washington's Capital One Arena, parents like Lisa Ramos, and even players like Lincoln Brown and Sarah Nurse, the presence of someone who looks like you and shares a cultural background with you in the same space as you—whether that's on the ice or in the rink, the front office, or the stands—can make all the difference in the world. Building a hockey-based community developed by and for Black women creates opportunities to provide targeted support that traditional hockey culture doesn't offer to racialized folks, simply because it has never been a priority to care for marginalized communities.

"I think about you and what you're doing more than you can imagine," Joel tells me. "To have that outlet, and that community to reach out [to], and somebody in your community would know what skates to buy, know what stick to get. And, you know, just some days we were treated unfairly by coaches and referees so just to have a safe place to come to . . .

I must commend you and say thank you. What you're doing for those families is truly amazing. It's truly amazing."

I remind Joel that his mother has an open invitation to join us at any of our BGHC events.

"You know," he replies, "I've always said, I wish my mother was at a game with y'all, supporting. At home, she said, 'When all this COVID is done.'"

We will hold you to that, Mama Ward.

Even though the experiences that Joel Ward and his family endured during his junior hockey career took place more than two decades ago, the stories I hear from the current BGHC scholarship awardees and their parents are eerily similar. Michelle McLean, a hockey mom from London, Ontario, is someone who saw the gaps in her daughter's team leadership and answered the call.

When we talk, I start by asking Michelle about her heritage, as I do every person I speak to about their experiences as a marginalized person in hockey. She says she is Canadian, and then clarifies that she is not "Black Canadian" because that means something else to Canadians from the East Coast, and that her ancestors are West Indian. "Mostly from Trinidad and the UK," Michelle offers. Her daughter, TaliaRose Tamborro, received the first-ever Black Girl Hockey Club scholarship in the summer of 2020, as BGHC was just starting to work out program requirements and discern what we wanted to do as a non-profit organization focused on uplifting Black girls in hockey. Kiana Scott, Black girl hockey scout for the Erie Otters of the OHL, had reached out to Kwame Mason, producer of the Black hockey history film *Soul on Ice*. Kwame then connected me and Kiana, who told me about TaliaRose and a goalie giveaway that she had applied for.

In 2019, a Canadian junior hockey goalie named Mikael Kingo had decided to start an annual give away in which up-and-coming goalies could apply to receive equipment purchased with donated funds. In 2020, after a written application process, eleven-year-old TaliaRose of the London Devilettes hockey team was chosen, and Kwame and Kiana hoped that BGHC could get involved to help fund the equipment. As soon as BGHC received our federal non-profit status, my board and I got to figuring out what our scholarship requirements would look like and how best we might be able to help TaliaRose. After a few conversations with Mikael and his mother, Lisette, we decided to surprise both Michelle and TaliaRose with not only the equipment, but an entire experience introducing the family to BGHC—and really, the world. I will never forget the reaction of Michelle, the only Black mother on her daughter's team, who had already worked so hard to keep her kid in hockey. Little did I know at the time that the scholarship, the BGHC community, and Michelle's work within hockey were just the beginning.

After the murder of George Floyd, when even hockey started to take racism seriously, leadership within the sport began to look at how best to address diversity and inclusion narratives within their organizations. From Hockey Canada to the NHL, BIPOC engagement in hockey, particularly with Black folks, became a subject of focus and then concern. The policies to protect players from racial abuse just weren't there.

"A childhood friend of mine, who's the president of one of the hockey boards in Southwestern Ontario, Shannon Price, called me because she had an incident in her organization and she was not willing to put up with it," says Michelle. "She wanted to get all the hockey presidents and people that would listen to help put together some sort of new structure in the guidelines and objectives for our hockey leagues, sort of like a new guideline rulebook. There have to be some sort of rules around what is not allowed, so action can be taken. Because there's nothing written, it's really hard for coaches, parents, other teammates to take a stand, because they don't know what rules things fall under."

As the only Black parent of the only Black girl on the London Devilettes, Michelle understands that her insight is necessary in order to help create equitable policy for racialized players on the team, in the league, and ultimately within the Hockey Canada youth system. She also recognizes that the league and the parents cannot wait for something bad to happen before creating a safety net for BIPOC players. In order to create a safe experience for not only her own child but all the Black and brown kids who will come after TaliaRose, Michelle decided to get involved.

"I never really thought about it. Actually, I shouldn't say never really thought about it. I didn't *know* that there wasn't a defined policy. See, when I look at our policy and read it, it talks about behaviour. And I forget exactly what the paragraph is. But at the time I really didn't think that there needed to be anything further. And then when Shannon called me and told me about the incident, and she's like, there's no policy written around racism. We have a lot of First Nations people here, like a lot. Not even anything around a policy protecting First Nations? So, if you're not protecting First Nations, and you're not protecting Black people—who, let's face it, bear the brunt of the racist ideology, period—then who are you protecting? It sounds like you're protecting something else."

From the outside, it sounds like Hockey Canada, the governing body for a majority of Canadian youth hockey leagues, is protecting itself and the shareholders who make money off the organization. It is protecting young white men who are not held accountable for their actions. It is protecting the status quo, and the way things have always been done. But Michelle says it best: "Really, the only thing that we should care about when they are on the ice is our kids' safety, having fun, fairness, and equality for all." Without specific policies put in place to protect youth players from racism, Hockey Canada and USA Hockey will continue to treat each case of abuse as if it is an isolated incident, instead of looking at the systemic and institutionalized reasons for these attacks. What Michelle and her peers are working on is a way to hold the organization and its leaders accountable. If we look at the scope of hockey culture, policy is truly the best and perhaps only way to facilitate an authentic culture shift that will benefit the most marginalized players—particularly Black and Indigenous players. When organizational policy prohibiting racist language and actions toward its workers and stakeholders does not explicitly exist, it is because that organization does not take those types of activities seriously. Parents of BIPOC hockey players must measure the benefits of hockey—team-building skills, independence, perseverance—against the real harm that institutional negligence can cause these kids.

Every scholarship season, BGHC gathers as many committee members as we can to hold congratulatory calls with awardees and their parents, coaches, and anyone who wants to join in on their end. We do this each time we award scholarships, so at least three times a year, with multiple calls scheduled each round, depending on how many scholarships we've been able to finagle. Scheduling these calls is a logistical nightmare, but thanks to BGHC admin assistant Isabel Graham (who, Sarah Nurse once said, "holds it down") and a flexible group of committee members, we can usually get a few of us on each call. When anyone asks, the scholarship committee will say that this is the best part of the year, but in all honesty, it can also feel very heavy.

These meetings give my team a chance to gather important information, like how parents want the money sent or what a winner's goal song is, while allowing parents and players to begin to develop a sense of what the BGHC community looks and feels like. The goal of my team is to make sure the parents and players know that this is a space created for all of them to thrive. For many of the parents, the burden of race, gender, and hockey has been theirs alone to bear. If they are lucky, like Lisa Ramos, they have a community to lean on as their child grows into the hockey player they want to be. Other parents have had to navigate hockey culture in isolation, their family the only one of colour at the rink. Being the *only one* takes a toll.

With the scholarship calls, we want to help these parents realize they aren't the only ones. I am here. BGHC volunteers are here. There are other parents on the call who are part of this community too. "While you may feel like you're the only one," I tell each group, "you're not. There are a lot of us out here, and we are building something special." It's during these calls that some of the parents and players begin to let down the walls that have kept them safe at the rink. They begin to share their stories with each other and with us. I have wept real tears for the awardees who have shared in the group their negative experiences in hockey, some as young as eight years old. Often, at the end of the hour, it feels like I've been sitting on my therapist's couch, digging deep into ancestral wounds. Parents, players, and volunteers commiserate, laugh, and sometimes cry, but each conversation is meant to be a call to action.

We are building a community in which we ask that each person touched by our work intentionally uplift Black women on and off the ice. For Black hockey parents, this means uplifting one another. "Look around and see your community. Keep in touch!" I tell them. "Keep your kids in touch." For non-Black parents, it means not only acknowledging their privilege but using it to improve the landscape of hockey for Black girls.

For our scholarship winners, the message is simple. *Play hockey as long as you want to, we're here to support you as far as you want to take this—and even if you're done, you're part of the BGHC family now, you're not getting rid of us any time soon.*

You see, I may not be a hockey mom, but I'll claim the role of hockey auntie any day.

THE FUTURE ACES CREED

I will develop a positive **Attitude** toward all
people and toward my work.

I will develop my talents and **Ability** in
A   order that I may be helpful to society.

I will take **Action** with integrity.

I will take initiative to **Achieve** my goals
with honest and sincere effort.

I will **Cooperate** with and respect others by
seeking understanding with all people,
regardless of race, gender or beliefs.

C   I will demonstrate **Courage**, standing up for
what is right and speaking out against what
is wrong.

I will display **Confidence** in all my actions
without being arrogant.

I will show **Empathy** and consideration by
advancing the values that are important to
me and others.

E   I will set a good **Example** to others, taking
responsibility for my actions.

I will acquire the best **Education** within my
capability.

I will be of **Service** to others.

S   I will practice good **Sportsmanship** in all my
decisions, demonstrating fair play to all.

—*Herbert H. Carnegie*

ON BEING "THE FIRST"

Most Black folks involved in ice hockey know the story of Herb Carnegie. The oft-quoted line is that he was the greatest Black hockey player to never play in the NHL. When Herb was eighteen, Conn Smythe, who owned the Toronto Maple Leafs at the time, saw Herb play. Smythe famously said that he would pay $10,000 if someone could make Herb white, an acknowledgement that while Herb's playing was excellent, the colour of his skin made it so hockey would not accept him.

The experience hurt, but it didn't break Herb's spirit. In 1941, Herb and his brother, Ossie Carnegie, began playing alongside Manny McIntyre, the three of them making up the first all-Black line in semi-professional hockey. The media called them the "Black Aces," among other things of course, and the trio later played together in the Quebec Provincial Hockey League for a number of years. In 1948, the New York Rangers finally scouted Herb, but when they sent over an offer of $2,700 to play in the minors, Herb refused to take a pay cut—he had four children and was making more in the Quebec league.

This act of defiance absolved white hockey executives from dealing with the anti-Blackness that prevented Herb from obtaining a professional contract, and he never went to the Big Show. Herb retired from playing hockey in 1954, and the next year founded the Future Aces Hockey School, which focused not just on hockey skills but also on life and social lessons. In 1987, Herb launched the charitable side of the hockey school, the Herbert H. Carnegie Future Aces Foundation. The board consisted of Herb, his wife, Audrey, and their daughter Bernice. Together, the Carnegie family built a legacy of leadership, Black excellence, and philanthropy.

In 1996, Bernice and Herb Carnegie published a book about his life, *A Fly in a Pail of Milk: The Herb Carnegie Story*. For years after its initial publication, the book was out of print. I know, because I looked for it everywhere, but also refused to buy it from Amazon. I finally received a copy of a new edition in a gift bag at a Toronto Maple Leafs luncheon in 2022 called "Celebrating Black Women in Hockey," at which Bernice and I both said a few words and were first introduced to each other. I let it sit on my bookshelf for five months, until right before the posthumous Hockey Hall of Fame induction for Herb Carnegie in the fall of 2022. What I didn't know until I picked it up was that this edition included an additional one hundred pages entitled "Part Two: Life Lessons Passed on from Father to Daughter." In a modest first-person account, Bernice writes of working alongside her father and her own specific experiences in hockey. She doesn't shy away from describing the hardships of existing in hockey spaces as a Black woman during the 1980s and '90s, when there was no Kim Davis or Black Girl Hockey Club to advocate for her—only her father and his creed.

I reached out to Bernice in the hopes that we could talk about the book, her work, and the legacy she was creating in hockey right now. When she responded with an affirmative and we set a date to chat, I was initially surprised that she would take the time out of her busy schedule to sit down with me. Only a week after our interview, Bernice would be standing in front of the hockey community for her father's induction into the Hockey Hall of Fame in Toronto. What I was coming to understand was that, even at seventy-seven, Bernice had a work ethic that couldn't be beat, plus she truly cared about people and about hockey. So much so that she was making time to talk to me between getting her oil changed and her extended family arriving from all over the world before the HHOF induction weekend.

In the mid-90s, Bernice Carnegie took a leap of faith. She wanted to work full-time for her father's foundation after a disappointing few years working in financial planning. So she quit her job, and went to work for the Future Aces full-time. Not only did Bernice see an opportunity to build something special for the hockey community, but she also wanted to create a space where she could feel respected and cared for—tenets of both her father's philosophy and her own personal world view.

"I think you need to understand why I did it in the first place," Bernice says. "I was working with the government. It ended up not being such a pleasant experience. I was an executive assistant to a director, and I had my father's philosophy [the Future Aces Creed] on the back wall behind my desk, and not everybody was behaving that way. I called them out a few times, and they didn't like it. I never thought that other people could hurt me. I was an adult, thinking, you know, other people's opinions of me didn't matter. By the time I left that job, I was emotionally broken, and I said to myself, *I don't want to work for anybody anymore*. I had been working but taking time off to go and do Future Aces with my father. I thought, *No, I want to do this full-time*. So I took a whole year off and I just worked on Future Aces. And in the end, I ended up with ten to fifteen new schools in the project, sharing my father's story about his hockey career, about his experiences of racism, and how he navigated around them to be successful.

"So, at the end of the year, I went back to our board. I had been on the board because I had started the organization when my dad needed three people, and that was my mother, and me, and him. I said to the rest of the board, 'This is what's happened because I've been working on this full-time. But I still have a mortgage on my house. And so, would you like to go forward and give me a paid job to do this, or are we just going to go back to all being volunteers?' They loved what happened, so they decided to move forward."

That first year, Bernice received a $10,000 honorarium for her work. The next year, she had a salary of $20,000 and, with her background in finance, decided that along with her investments, she would have enough financial security to pay her bills. With her own children grown and out of the house, Bernice decided to pursue her lifelong passion of community-building in hockey using Herb Carnegie's philosophy.

"My father had been working in the community for such a long time and when I joined him, people loved it. They loved the father-family connection. We became constant companions; it was kind of like we were joined at the hip. When I got really involved in Future Aces, my father was going blind, actually, at that time. So I was the lead person to develop the foundation into what it became. It had an educational component, where we went out to schools, and we trained teachers on how to take the values that my father had created and actually apply [them] to life. So people were very accepting of our story, because the story was not only about my father and our life, but about them. Because it was trying to help other people to find the best of who they could be. But we did it through storytelling, and sharing how my father wound his life around the obstacles to become that better person."

Bernice Carnegie is a trailblazer. While her father may have been *the first*, Bernice broke barriers by existing in hockey spaces as a Black woman, an executive, and a leader while continuing to create spaces for marginalized folks in hockey using the values set forth in her father's Future Aces Creed. Community-building in hockey involves putting time, energy, and money into organizations that work toward the mission of inclusivity and equity for all. Bernice uses her knowledge, her connections, and her name to amplify the work of those that follow her father's creed—most recently the Carnegie Initiative, a non-profit co-founded by Bernice and Bryant McBride, which aims to ensure opportunity and access to hockey for all. In 2020, I was asked to sit on the board of directors of the Carnegie Initiative, and I currently work with the organization as a volunteer. Taking on this position wasn't something I did lightly, but I joined trusting that its purpose and vision mirrored not only those of BGHC, but Bernice and Herb's own Future Aces.

"The Carnegie Initiative is a special place. We have an opportunity to actually share stories that inspire people to be the best of who they can be," said Bernice. "That was one of the things that we were trying to do when we announced our Herbert Carnegie Trailblazer Award. We can let millions of people know that there are people out there working to do the right thing. Yes, there are problems, but there are also people who are trying to solve the problems, and we need to share those stories."

The Herbert Carnegie Trailblazer Award announced its inaugural class in 2022, with seven recipients from throughout North America who were recognized as exemplifying Herbert Carnegie's work and legacy:

- Alexandria Briggs-Blake, Tucker Road Ducks
- Kirk Brooks, Seaside Hockey and Skillz Hockey
- Stephane Friday, Hockey Indigenous
- Moezine Hasham, Hockey 4 Youth
- Nathaniel Mata, RGV Roller
- Brock McGillis, LGBTQ activist
- Zarmina Nekzai, Hockey Girls of Kabul

These individuals and organizations have missions that combat bigotry in hockey, and my personal goals and values align with so much of the work that they do. In my work with BGHC, I've collaborated with a few of the folks listed above, and I am excited to learn more about the others.

"We have an opportunity to further develop them and to share with other people. So that we can help each other," says Bernice. "You don't always have to reinvent the wheel, you can borrow . . . from other organizations things that are working. It's not stealing. It's borrowing. Because once somebody creates something that works, why wouldn't you want to share it with others? That's exactly what my father did. He shared it with others, and he taught me to do the same thing. So I really do feel like I'm standing on his shoulders, I really do feel like I've learned a lot of the lessons. One of the things that I'm proud of is that I actually listened to my father, because we don't always listen to our parents. Well, I listened enough to learn that what he was doing had value for everybody."

Bernice Carnegie's vision for her father's Future Aces Foundation continues with the Carnegie Initiative. Using storytelling, community spaces, and a staunch set of values based on integrity and equality for all, the Carnegie family, with Bernice at the head, continues to influence the larger hockey community in a positive way.

"There's nothing I'm doing with the Carnegie Initiative that I didn't do before. I am the conscience of the organization that keeps tapping, tapping, tapping our members on the head, and going, *Okay, so we just heard a lot of crap. Now, we're going to be the higher ideal, we're not going to sink to that level, we're going to actually find a way to bring us to a higher level.* I'm proud of the group that we're working with, and our meetings every week are positive in that we get to laugh and smile while we talk about how we make those changes."

In order for BIPOC to create space for others in hockey, we must love the game with intentionality. For Bernice, that means building an inclusive community that reminds us that we are not alone—and nor are we "the only one." There are others all over the world who are working toward similar goals, experiencing similar joys and struggles, in solidarity. When we work together, we can accomplish so much more.

For Black women in sports, the "firsts" continue to happen. Many of those firsts in ice hockey were achieved by Blake Bolden. In 2013, Blake was the first African American drafted into the CWHL, when she was selected in the first round by the Boston Blades. Blake played with the league until spring 2015, when she helped her team win the Clarkson Cup. In 2015, Blake joined the NWHL's Boston Pride, and became the first African American player to compete in the newly formed league. In 2016, Blake helped the Pride win the inaugural Isobel Cup. After a very disappointing omission from the U.S. national team, Blake moved to Switzerland to play with HC Lugano. She subsequently became the first Black female scout for the NHL, working with the Los Angeles Kings, and created for herself the club's—and the league's—first diversity and inclusion specialist position. We can even clock some of her "firsts" happening before Blake played professional hockey. She attended Northwood School, a boarding school in Lake Placid, and shockingly enough was the only Black student. Not just on her hockey team, or in her grade, but at the entire school, for four long years.

Let that sink in.

Thankfully, Blake takes her historic role as a Black hockey icon in stride.

"When I was, let's see, twenty-four, twenty-five years old in the CWHL, I realized that I was a role model. I hadn't realized that before. I knew that I wanted to become one; I knew when I was six years old I wanted to be the first Black U.S. Olympic national team player for the women, but I didn't know how to get there. I didn't know who could be my mentor. I didn't have any role models. I was just taking experiences as I went and just trying to be the best person that I could be at that time as I was playing."

I'm interviewing Blake in 2020, but this isn't the first time we've spoken. In fact, I credit Blake with giving me the spark of confidence to move forward with the concept of Black Girl Hockey Club during a conversation we had back in 2018. To be a hundred per cent honest, I consider the *very* first time I interviewed Blake to be one of my most unprofessional moments as a writer, and I dread revisiting it, but I'm trying to practise what I preach when it comes to transparency and vulnerability. It's important to understand how vulnerable Blake and I, as well as other Black women working in hockey, must be (especially with one another) in order to build authentic and inclusive spaces.

Back in 2018, when BGHC was just a hope and a dream, sports journalist and colleague Erica Ayala suggested I reach out to Blake. She even vouched for my character so that Blake would agree to hop on a call and chat with me about Black folks in hockey. I had notes and questions for Blake because, even back then, I had this book in mind. I set up the recorder, and when she joined the Skype call that spring afternoon in 2018, we had a couple of stops and starts until I got over being star-struck enough to press record and ask my questions. About thirty minutes in, the conversation began to feel more private and personal, and as I checked my notes and mentally went over my talking points, I realized, mortified, that I'd never told her I was recording. I interrupted her in the middle of a sentence, finally, and, red-faced, confessed I had been recording the entire conversation. I stumbled over my words, embarrassed and a little terrified of my misstep. If I planned to engage with other hockey folks this way, how could they ever trust me if this was my level of professionalism in these spaces? But Blake was so incredibly gracious, my god—and she didn't have to be. She allowed me to continue recording, and I vowed to keep the information private, regardless of permissions, because I didn't want her to feel coerced.

That day set the tone for my future work and how I engage with Black folks in hockey. Mindfulness and intentionality go a long way, particularly when I'm working with Black women. So does admitting when I'm wrong. The incident, along with Blake's kindness and her trust in me, solidified the fact that I would do anything to make her and players like her, with similar experiences and backgrounds, feel safe in hockey. I wanted to create a space where we could trust each other, even through our mistakes. When we do that, we grow.

The path Bernice, Blake, and other Black women are forging in this sport is not an easy one to travel. In order to maintain her personal values, Blake makes sure that each partnership she creates and job she takes on matches the energy she intends to bring to Black hockey communities everywhere, including BGHC. It's humbling to be on the good side of Blake's set of values, and the day we first met I recognized that if I could do my work with even a modicum of the grace and thoughtfulness that she exudes in her day-to-day dealings, I would be doing something meaningful for the sport of hockey.

"I usually don't do things that don't feel natural or good for me," Blake tells me. "So if I do it, I feel like that's a positive step for not only myself, but just visibility for Black people in the sport of ice hockey. So I take these opportunities and I gobble them up. For instance, on the NHL Player Inclusion Committee [now Coalition], that was really scary for me, because I was basically presenting to the Executive Inclusion Council—Gary Bettman, Kim Davis, and all the other presidents and owners of teams involved—about how they need to do their job better. And that was scary, right? It's not even, *You need to do your job better.* It's just, *This is from my perspective, and my experiences, and this is how I would like to see change,* and they were open to it. That was awesome."

As a member of the NHL's Player Inclusion Coalition, the first (and so far only) Growth and Inclusion Specialist for the Los Angeles Kings, and one of the first Black Girl Hockey Club supporters, Blake Bolden is *the first* (pun intended) to admit that she is not a DEI specialist by training. What she does have is lived experience, a stellar hockey IQ, and an intrinsic understanding of how to navigate the very delicate hockey ecosystem in order to achieve her goals. She also works hard to be a changemaker alongside people who share her values. Blake moves through hockey spaces with intentionality, connecting, supporting, and engaging with those who want hockey to be the best sport it can be for each and every marginalized person. "I'm not an expert in a lot of things besides hockey," she confesses. "So I always just follow my heart with those sorts of things and support the people that I feel need it."

Blake's heart has led her to develop a strong support community around her, including Canadian Olympic hockey player Sarah Nurse. The two have similar stories when it comes to their hockey careers, but at the time of my conversation with Blake, they had never met in person. For Blake, Sarah is someone with whom she shares a kinship, not just because of hockey but because of their cultural background and the unique space they have occupied, even as they did so in different national programs. "Sarah and I have never met," Blake says. "I've never met the girl in my entire life. But she and I understand each other from a distance. It doesn't really matter if I've never shaken her hand or given her a hug; I feel as though we've already done that because of the support we've given each other."

That support looks like the two of them staying in touch even when they're not at the same events, and checking in on one another when times get tough. For Sarah Nurse, the support has been invaluable and a recent development in a lifelong hockey career. Playing at the highest level of hockey for Canada, Sarah admits to often feeling alone and isolated. With no other Black women *in the world* playing Olympic-level hockey, Sarah knows what it's like to be the only Black girl in the room, but in April 2022 that changed when she came to her very first in-person Black Girl Hockey Club event in Toronto, Ontario.

In February 2022, Sarah Nurse and the Canadian women's hockey team won a gold medal at the Beijing Olympics. That made Sarah the first Black woman to ever win gold in hockey for any country, ever. Now, my own relationship with Sarah goes back to early 2020, when I reached out to ask her to join the first-ever digital Black Girl Hockey Club meet-up, right after the coronavirus pandemic locked down the world. Delvina Morrow and Tracey McCants Lewis from the Pittsburgh Penguins helped BGHC get online and do one of those Zoom parties everyone eventually came to hate. But during the early days of the pandemic, folks seemed to be looking for human connection and community. As Sarah helped to cultivate the Black Girl Hockey Club community by attending our virtual event, she also treasured the space and began to show her support of our organization publicly. She posted a picture of herself wearing a BGHC sweatshirt on her personal Instagram feed, and talked about the impact of the organization to the media.

Sarah Nurse is incredibly down-to-earth, and in some ways a typical hockey player. Her collegiate background in business marketing and her public relations training with the Canadian national program has given her a framework within which she navigates the hockey landscape. As a player, Sarah has done something no other Black woman has accomplished, ever. Her place on the Canadian national women's hockey team has been secured through not only her incredible play, but her ability to fit into the mould of what Hockey Canada wants from its national players, the majority of whom are white. Sarah has a large social media following, and as she gets older, with more high-level experience under her belt, she has started to utilize her platform to speak out against injustices that matter to her. Sarah uses her voice and shares her story with other Black women—as well as those watching us grow in this space—in order to help create a more equitable sport for all.

"Obviously I'm very aware that I have lighter skin, I have a lighter complexion. I know people use the term *white passing* a lot. I don't love that term because, although I have lighter skin, I've never been able to walk into somewhere and people say, 'Oh, she's white.' They're always like, 'Oh, where are you from?' I've always been, in this kind of sense, Other," Sarah admits.

"I feel like a lot of people don't know how to approach that. I've been privy to different conversations and comments that, if I had darker skin, I would not have been privy to, you know? Being told, 'You're not THAT Black. So don't be offended by these things.' And it's like, what does that really mean?" she asks, albeit rhetorically, because she and I both know what it means. Colourism dictates that the lighter the skin of someone of African descent (or any race, really), the greater their proximity to whiteness, and therefore the less they can (or should) identify with Blackness. This creates a false sense of belonging to white culture and an alienation from Black culture. It's a lose-lose situation, really, but it can be enticing to some.

So, how does Sarah Nurse quantify her Blackness? Well, she let me know from the beginning of our conversation that she's biracial. Sarah has light skin and soft curls that may make her teammates and the rest of the hockey world believe that if she is *less* Black than someone with darker skin, like Mikyla Grant-Mentis or P.K. Subban. She is not. For Sarah, engaging with Black fans and players has become an intentional act that has given her a sense of freedom in hockey spaces that she didn't have a few years ago.

"I can't say that I've had people saying hateful things to me directly. But hearing them about my family, about my friends, was always very difficult to me and put me in a very uncomfortable position. Because I'm just like, *Well, what do I do here?*

"I think that I've even had a unique privilege in the sense that, because I excel at hockey, I am afforded more respect, whereas if I just play hockey for fun, as a biracial girl, I probably wouldn't have been afforded that respect, I probably wouldn't have made friends that easily, you know? I know that I have a privilege because I excelled at what I do. Whereas other women of colour, who, you know, may not be a national team talent, are not afforded the same respect."

While the acknowledgement of her own light-skinned privilege is a step in the right direction, Sarah knows it doesn't stop there. She must also use that privilege to create change in her own environment. Standing up for herself hasn't always been easy, but Sarah admits that she works every day not only to understand her own background and culture but to speak up when folks weaponize Blackness against her.

"As I've gotten older, and more, I guess, confident in myself and my knowledge, I've been a lot more willing to stand up and confront in those situations, because obviously, especially when you're feeling like you're the only one who really understands what's going on, you're not really encouraged to stand up and say, 'Hey, I didn't love that comment.' When I was younger, a lot of the time it was like, *I don't feel comfortable right now, but I don't actually know why*. Right? And so I feel like, now that I know the roots [of those comments] and how [they make] me feel, it's easier for me to stand up."

As Sarah begins to unpack the ways that anti-Blackness affects her life and work, she does so with the support of her family, her friends, and, of course, Black Girl Hockey Club. When she travelled to Beijing in February 2022 for the Winter Olympics with the Canadian women's national hockey team, Sarah did so with an entire community behind her. That winter, I did some broadcast work with CBC Sports, a division of the Canadian Broadcasting Corporation, and got to go on television and talk about women's Olympic hockey alongside Shireen Ahmed, who is a CBC correspondent living in Toronto and one of my best friends. I'd never done broadcast work before and it wasn't something I'd ever really thought about doing. That being said, I had a blast recording a few segments for *The Extra Hour* with Brendan Dunlop and Alex Despatie. It took me a couple of tries to get going, but the production team at CBC made sure I felt comfortable and had a good time while on the air.

I spent hours researching women's Olympic hockey history while watching the 2022 Games in order to have a few intelligent things to say in those five-minute segments. I am not partial to nationalism, but as the only American on a Canadian broadcast, I did spend my fair share of time talking about the very skilled U.S. women's hockey team, with the hope that I could claim bragging rights among my Canadian friends if the U.S. won gold again. Throughout the tournament, though, the breakout star of the games, for me anyway, happened to be Sarah Nurse, on the Canadian side. Aside from becoming the first Black woman to win Olympic ice hockey gold, Sarah recorded 18 points in the tournament, surpassing Hall of Fame legend Hayley Wickenheiser's 17 points at the 2006 Olympics. Even as I cheered for Team USA, I couldn't help but let CBC (and the world) know that, this time, I was rooting for the only Black girl playing hockey at the Olympics. And then she won gold!!!

When Sarah Nurse won, I couldn't help but feel pride in her accomplishments as a Black woman hockey player in a space that had never intended for her to excel in such a unique and important way. As we came off the high of that Olympic win for all Black girl hockey fans, I was actually planning an event in Toronto with the Maple Leafs and other Black-women-led organizations in the GTA (Greater Toronto Area), and I decided to shoot my shot and invite Sarah, who is from Toronto, to join us.

I had just started working with some Black folks in the Maple Leafs organization on a panel event we called the "Brilliant Blackness of Women in Hockey," with Dayton O'Donoghue, a local hockey player and two-time BGHC scholarship awardee; Raegan Subban, digital and social media content creator for TSN and BarDown; and Saroya Tinker, professional hockey player for the Toronto Six and soon-to-be executive director of BGHC Canada. When I asked Sarah to join the panel, she was actually overseas still, doing the rounds and celebrating the gold medal win with her teammates. Her response was only two lines, and she hadn't even changed her email signature from "Olympic Silver medallist" yet, but she accepted the invitation, and BGHC got started on planning an event with a newly minted gold medal winner.

In Toronto, when we finally met, it was as if we were old friends. She immediately began to joke and chat with me and the young girls and their families, as well as the many fans in attendance, and she seemed so warm and down-to-earth. The panel was one-of-a-kind, featuring Black women working in a variety of roles in hockey. We were not focused on trauma or the ways that racism had negatively affected us, although at times those stories came up. Instead, we spent our time celebrating Black joy, Black women, and Black accomplishments in hockey. My vision for this kind of work and BGHC as a whole lies in community, celebrating each other, and uplifting our individual and collective accomplishments in order to create not just a safe space for Black women in hockey, but a haven that nurtures and encourages growth. So many of us may be the first of our kind in this sport—but that does not mean we will be the last.

"I still get goosebumps thinking about that day," Sarah Nurse tells me later that year. We're on a video call—I'm in Ohio for my sister's wedding, while Sarah is in her home in Toronto. "I understand how impactful that was on them, but also on myself as well." When I ask her about a memorable moment during the day, she blows me away with her response.

"Meeting Dayton, and some of the other girls, was just really, really special because they have these dreams, they have big dreams, they have wide eyes. You know, they're so young, they're so full of energy and the fact that I could come home and share a gold medal and think about them doing that one day is so special. Just being surrounded by the other Black women, by the other BIPOC women as well, was absolutely incredible. And it's so long overdue, for sure," she says.

"We deserve a spot in that space. It's been such a long time coming and not only as players but obviously as fans, as people in the media, as people working corporate [or] social media. I think that that was really inspiring, to listen to Raegan [Subban] speak about what she does, and her journey and her obviously pretty awesome family in the sports world as well. But her just carving out a space for herself in a place that's not normally seen as for Black women. And so it was just amazing to see so many people in that space who are taking their rightful spots.

"I remember speaking to a group of Muslim women who told me about how they had started like a Muslim ball hockey team, I believe, and they were the only ones, and you know, they never saw women wearing hijabs. And so the fact that they were like, *We're just so inspired by you and what you're doing . . .*"

Not one to hog the spotlight, Sarah made sure she took the time to remind the girls of their importance in these same spaces. The Azmi sisters are hijabi, from Toronto, and really quite good at ball hockey. They joined BGHC at MLSE LaunchPad, the Maple Leafs' youth sports centre, in solidarity with our work. When Sarah met the sisters, she wanted to make sure that they understood the impact that they would continue to have in hockey spaces.

"I was like, you have to understand that what you're doing is being a representative. You are shedding light and being somebody that little Muslim girls can look up to as well. The change in their face was just like, *Yeah, we're doing that too.* It's understanding that we as Black women and people of underrepresented communities in the hockey world are all representatives. It's not just me, who has been to the Olympics. It is literally everybody in this space. I think turning that around on them was really empowering. It was awesome to see. They were amazing to talk to."

It's powerful to hear the most accomplished Black woman hockey player in the world say that by simply existing in hockey spaces, people like the Azmi sisters are creating radical change. It means that she realizes that the power she and the rest of us hold comes from just being ourselves. For women like Sarah, Blake, Bernice, and myself, that means intentionally uplifting those with the least power, sharing the lessons passed down to us by our ancestors, and working toward goals that benefit communities in need. It means taking care of ourselves so that we can take care of our communities, and betting on ourselves and our own skill sets in order to best give back to those same communities.

In November 2022, I travelled to Toronto to knock out a few work-related activities. First, the Carnegie Initiative hosted a closed-door symposium with the GTHL (Greater Toronto Hockey League) and the NHL. Not many Americans sat in on the event, so I took the opportunity to listen and learn about the hockey landscape in Canada, just as we prepared for the launch of BGHC Canada. The HHOF induction for Herb Carnegie and the rest of the class of 2022 was only a week after this symposium, and so Saroya Tinker and I worked to time the BGHC Canada organizational launch to take place in between the two events.

With the support of Canadian Tire's charity organization, Jumpstart, and its president, Marco Di Buono, we pulled together an event for GTA scholarship awardees and mentees as well as BGHC supporters, giving them the chance to participate in wellness activities, get free hockey gear, and meet other Black hockey families in the area. I extended an invitation to Bernice Carnegie, knowing full well that she most likely would be too busy to attend because of all the HHOF festivities. Although I didn't get to see her, I was pleasantly surprised to hear that she stopped by our launch event to show her public support and to encourage us in our shared mission to make hockey a more welcoming space for all.

But for me, that week in Canada was one of the most difficult of the entire year. I arrived exhausted and harried, mentally unprepared for a cold, wet fall season in Toronto. I'd left my home life tumultuous, and spent most of my evenings in Toronto talking to folks back in California, trying to straighten out some of the personal drama that was unfolding. I didn't have any cell service or a car, which made day travel confusing and a little scary. My friend Shireen and I had a lovely spa day early on in the trip, but I ran off into the rain immediately after to sit in on another meeting, which I didn't allow myself to slow down enough to enjoy. The BGHC Canada launch day events were fun, but the constant go-going got to me, and I woke up on Sunday morning with a pretty bad eye infection and a sore throat, feeling homesick and sad. I ended up having to make some difficult choices in order to take care of my own physical well-being, cancelling plans to attend the Carnegie celebration dinner and missing the induction ceremony as well. And I'd wanted to get dressed up so badly!

After travelling across international borders in order to accomplish a number of work goals and making commitments to folks I respect, I ended up spending the last two and a half days of my trip in my hotel room, crying, ordering food, and watching old Paul Newman movies instead of showing up and showing out for BGHC. When I got home, I felt defeated. I made a doctor's appointment, got some antibiotics, and slowly started the process of healing my body and my soul. But I couldn't shake the feeling that I had failed myself, and the stress began to manifest itself physically. I couldn't seem to get well, and thoughts of inadequacy and imposter syndrome began to seep in as I saw how my Canadian colleagues were doing the hard work in hockey while my organization continued to struggle to find sustainable partnerships. It meant the world to me when I opened up my email just a few days after American Thanksgiving to a message from Bernice Carnegie. She had missed me at the HHOF induction ceremony activities and wanted to make sure I had gotten home safely and that I was feeling better. While the thoughtfulness in her kind email did not stop me from being sad or stressed, it did remind me that there are leaders out there who have had similar experiences as me, who care about me, and who want to see me succeed.

The genuine care that women like Bernice, Blake, and Sarah have for the people they encounter continues to astound me. The authenticity and intentionality behind their words and their work inspire me as a Black woman, but also touch each and every person who sees what they have done for hockey and who strives to do the same. This is how trailblazers operate when they want to build inclusive spaces for all marginalized folks. This is Herb Carnegie's Future Aces at work, in a world that not only doesn't want to see people like me in a space like hockey, but actively works against it.

It isn't easy being the first—the first Black woman to win gold, to run a hockey school, to be a professional hockey scout, to start a hockey non-profit that values Black women above all else. "Firsts" need the support and care of our communities. But by creating safe spaces where others can be vulnerable and honest, we give ourselves that same gift—and that's a beautiful thing to behold.

WOHO AND WHITE FEMINISM

I'm equal parts excited and terrified to write about WoHo. For one, I'm not an expert, by any means. Sure, I got the chance to go on the CBC during the 2022 Winter Olympics and talk women's hockey, but I did meticulous research for each of my five-minute segments and still can't name-drop many women's hockey players off the top of my head. I didn't even know what MPP (Marie-Philip Poulin) stood for when I first heard the acronym! I had to think about it for a sec. I'm embarrassed, truly.

In addition to my lack of knowledge, women's hockey has historically been woefully difficult to find on television, and in terms of live games, the furthest west the Premier Hockey Federation (PHF) ever went is to Minnesota, and the newly formed Professional Women's Hockey League (PWHL) looks to have the same borders in mind. We don't have college hockey for women in California, either. In fact, the only women's hockey games I've been to are the 2019 National Women's Hockey League (NWHL) All-Star Game in Nashville, and the 2022 U.S. vs. Canada showcase in L.A., hosted by friends of

BGHC the Los Angeles Kings. Oh, and a women's world championship game in Canada, in the midst of writing this chapter, which we will get to later.

Like other WoHo fans in the U.S., I've mostly used the box scores, social media, and fan accounts to keep up with the hockey girlies, because there haven't always been a lot of options. In 2021, the PHF brokered a deal with ESPN+ that offered the first season-long coverage of women's hockey, from the beginning of the season to the Isobel Cup Final game. When the PHF was bought out by the PWHL in 2023, a new deal was cut, this time with CBC in Canada and WSN (Women's Sports Network) in the U.S. The league's high-quality broadcasts are also available for free to watch on YouTube live. While broadcast exposure is a big deal for the PWHL, it's important to remember that independent media companies like Black Rosie Media and the Ice Garden have done much of the heavy lifting in terms of consistent coverage of WoHo. Many high-profile sports entertainment companies seem to only highlight women's sports when there is a controversy or a championship. With Canada's most prominent news company invested in hockey's new women's league, the future is bright and broadcast weekly all season long for us hockey fans. Still, it's important to understand and respect the past of women's hockey in order to build a flourishing future.

So, undertaking the task (that I gave myself) to write about WoHo means I get to potentially introduce you, dear reader, to the wonderful world of women's sports, and reiterate why it's so important to invest in women, while also addressing the specific challenges that Black women face in these spaces. Yes, we are talking about white feminism!

Of course, women athletes want to play sports, not address intersectional identities. At least not all the time. We see the disparities: reporters asking women about their kids and not asking the men; commenting on women's clothing and looks, but not the men's. Women don't have the luxury of ignoring gender bias or misogyny, and Black women, Black *queer* women, *Black trans women*, have multiple intersections that are often called into question and discriminated against, even by other women.

Back in 2016, I started using women's hockey as an example of wage disparity in a freshman English class that I taught at the time called "Argument Writing." It was also a low-key introduction to the concept of feminism for these college freshmen. In this lesson, we specifically went over the differing governing models within women's hockey, as well as ways in which women athletes have had to fight for equal treatment compared to men. When in 2017 the U.S. women's hockey team announced they were going to boycott the International Ice Hockey Federation (IIHF) Women's World Championship, after negotiations with USA Hockey for support equal to the men's team came to a standstill, my class went over the tangible disparities, such as flights and hotel accommodations, game tickets for family members, and livable wages. In women's hockey, these inequities led to the creation of multiple financial models, with leaders who truly care about the sport hoping to find a way to make women's hockey sustainable in the same way that we see happening for sports like women's basketball. Unlike the WNBA—the women's league counterpart to the NBA that launched in 1996—women's hockey has never received full backing from its men's league counterpart, the NHL, and according to commissioner Gary Bettman it probably never will.

The various financial models of women's hockey—seen in the now-defunct Canadian Women's Hockey League (CWHL) and NWHL/PHF, as well as the Professional Women's Hockey Players Association (PWHPA), which morphed into the PWHL in 2023—have been continuously scrutinized and picked apart by media companies, other professional leagues, and "fans" with no intention of supporting women's hockey in any meaningful way. And that's just the sexism! For Black women who play hockey, the stakes become even higher. Racism, misogynoir, and microaggressions are commonplace in hockey.

When I launched Black Girl Hockey Club, I had very little knowledge about the complexities of women's hockey, outside of what I had researched with my students. My original entry point to hockey was the men's professional league, and I learned about women's sports issues from the women playing and from their fans. Mainstream sports media does not cover women's hockey like they do men's hockey, and hockey is fourth on the list of America's favourite sports, anyway. The information is there, if you know where to look, but if you're a casual hockey fan, CBC and WSN are locked in *now*—everybody else, not so much. It's a frustration for fans and players alike. Building a sustainable professional league, creating infrastructure, and securing funding for women's hockey hasn't been easy, but the passion for the game and the tremendous skill are there.

Established in 2007 as a senior league in the Greater Toronto Area, Montreal, and Ottawa, for twelve seasons the Canadian Women's Hockey League was known as the highest level of women's hockey in North America. Operating within a co-op financial system that included splitting costs and revenue evenly among the players (during good years and lean ones), the CWHL paid its players stipends only during the last two seasons, and dissolved in 2019 after financial troubles and a loss of viewership.

When the National Women's Hockey League launched in 2015, it did so as the first-ever women's professional league to pay its players a salary, although it was not a livable wage. In 2021, the NWHL changed its name to the Premier Hockey Federation to reflect the gender diversity of professional hockey, and by 2023 players earned a minimum salary of $62,285. Still, in May 2019, the low pay and lack of sufficient health benefits prompted more than 200 players from both the CWHL and the NWHL to release a joint statement announcing their intent not to participate in any North American professional league for the 2019–20 season. That same month, those players formed the Professional Women's Hockey Players Association, a non-profit dedicated to advocating for the promotion of professional women's ice hockey.

The 2019–20 season was the first of the ongoing strike by the players, and the beginning of the famed PWHPA showcase tournaments. For the following season, the PWHPA organized into five different hubs, each of which fielded a roster that competed in exhibition games across North America and in the Dream Gap tour tournament against each other. While the PHF drafted stellar players like Kelsey Koelzer, Saroya Tinker, and Mikyla Grant-Mentis, the PWHPA was where players like Sarah Nurse, Hilary Knight, and MPP set their sticks. And then, in the summer of 2023, the PHF folded and the Professional Women's Hockey League was born out of the PWHPA.

Yeah. It's very complicated—like, telenovela-complicated.

Dissolving the PHF for the PWHL created one league: a unified professional organization for women to play hockey in after college. But in truth, not all WoHo fans wanted a combined league. The PWHPA has historically been made up of elite, Olympic-calibre players, and many felt as if combining with the PHF would dilute the talent and tilt the ice. Others find the concept of a league fed mostly by national team players exclusionary to those who haven't had success in the national system for a variety of reasons, including racism in a business that may have a high number of women leaders, but, let's be honest, is run by white people.

Most often, the conversation around women playing professional hockey centres gender identity and quality of product, with little mind paid to non-white representation at the highest levels. Much like men's hockey, women's professional hockey is racially homogeneous. As the daughter of a Chinese immigrant father and a biracial (Puerto Rican and Chinese) mother, Julie Chu was the very first non-white person to skate with Team USA, starting back in 2000. Abby Roque, who won silver at the 2022 Beijing Olympics and was the first Indigenous woman on Team USA, is the only other non-white woman to currently play at the highest levels of hockey in the United States.

Black girls have started to infiltrate the national team systems, however, slowly but surely. Chicago native Noa Diop won a BGHC scholarship in fall 2022 after deciding to live and play in France with the hopes of making the French national team. Laila Edwards, Black girl hockey player from the

University of Wisconsin–Madison, began her journey on the American women's team in fall 2023, during the U.S. vs. Canada Rivalry Series. While these two players work to gain the chance to represent their countries in the Olympics one day, they are a visible symbol of the changing demographics of the sport—as well as the stark reality that only a single Black woman, Sarah Nurse, BGHC friend and gold medallist for Team Canada, has ever played Olympic hockey for any country, ever.

White feminism will tell us that there are certain inter-sections that are more important than others, and that equality is tiered. It starts with eradicating sexism, and at some point the misogyny and racism experienced by non-white women are pushed aside in favour of making sure that "all girls" get the chance to succeed. White feminism will girlboss its way into capitalist systems, which are based in white supremacy and built so that marginalized communities fail. While these systems are created and designed for white men, an implicit understanding of white feminism is that these same structures should benefit white women, as long as they continue to exclude non-white people. Dreama Moon and Michelle Holling, professors at California State University, San Marcos, wrote in their 2020 piece for *Communication and Critical/Cultural Studies*: "(White) feminism ideologically grounds itself in a gendered victimology that masks its participation and functionality in white supremacy. By erasing women of color, positioning women as victims of white male hegemony, and failing to hold white women accountable for the production and reproduction of white supremacy, (white) feminism manifests its allegiance to whiteness and in doing so commits 'discursive violence.'"

I have a lot of conversations with women of colour about white feminism, but this concept is a very touchy subject and I often find it difficult to have meaningful conversations with white women about white feminism without bringing about "white woman tears" and causing them to act defensively. I work in higher education, which has been a dream of mine since I graduated high school. I always kind of wanted to teach college-aged students literature and writing, but when I graduated with my master's in lit, I realized that even at my alma mater there weren't a lot of teaching jobs available, let alone faculty positions, and I couldn't afford to go another $100k into debt for a Ph.D. in the hopes that something might open up. So I kept my day job in an administrative position at the university, taught writing courses as an adjunct professor, and built BGHC in my time off. No shit.

Over the decade that I've worked at the university, there have been fewer than a dozen Black women in positions of power on my campus. Because I am one of two people who work in my department, even though I am *only* staff and not faculty (without that Ph.D., *shame*), I am salaried, and I suppose would be considered by some to hold a position of authority. Unfortunately, this has led to conflict, and something I have noticed—colloquially of course—is that when I tell white women "no" they get real, real mad. I mean, *m-a-d* enough to tell me I'm bad at my job, to yell at me, to undercut me, to talk about me when I'm not around, to go over my head, and to aggressively ignore me at any and all university functions and even in the hallways we share. I have experienced this behaviour from women twice my age, who have more degrees, more money, more access, and more privilege than they know what to do with, but it's odd, white feminism. The lack of self-reflection and subsequent victimization leads directly to "discursive violence"—behaviours, decisions, and strategies that are products of anti-Blackness.

In a 2018 article for *Harper's Bazaar*, Rachel Cargle broke down a few common examples of the discursive violence of white feminism: *tone policing*—where the words *could* be impactful, if we would only make them more palatable; *spiritual bypassing*—when "love and light" turns into a way to ignore the realities of racism; *white saviour complex*—focusing on how to "fix" social issues for others instead of doing the inner work; and *centring*, which is at the middle of all of these and is all about how white women *feel* about racial issues. Cargle goes on to write that "many liberal white women have an immediate reaction of defense when someone challenges their intentions. And it is in that precise moment they need to stop and realize they are actually part of the problem."

In the decade-plus that I have been working in higher education, I've come to understand white feminism more than I would like. I have come to realize that even just doing my job by the book can piss people off, and how harmful the discursive violence borne of white feminism can be to my professional growth as well as my mental health. For years, I laboured under white women in positions of power, not realizing the impact that discursive violence had on me internally and professionally until I started working for a Black male boss who supported me in ways I never imagined possible! Looking back, I see the ways and the reasons why my confidence had been chipped away by the insidious white feminism of higher education, and I refuse to have those same experiences in hockey—my second career, and my passion.

I come to hockey spaces as my whole authentic self, speaking aloud about concepts like white supremacy and misogynoir in order to combat what I haven't had success fighting against in some of the other spaces I occupy. My desire to take up space in higher education has lessened over the years, because higher education is a bastion of privilege and access, and I find that I am no longer interested in spending money to make money, waiting my turn, or being relegated to second-class status because I don't have enough letters after my name. I am no longer interested in justifying my humanity, my weaknesses, or my strengths in order to satisfy white supremacist structures. I am picking my battles carefully, and moving up the ladder of higher education just isn't something I'm willing to fight for any longer. Instead, I focus my activism on hockey and the spaces that I have helped to create there for Black and marginalized women.

In my time interviewing folks for this book, I had a lot of conversations that didn't make the cut and a few that I come back to time and time again. One is the chat I had with Sarah Nurse after her 2022 Olympic gold medal win. Like most of the top national players, Sarah is a member of the PWHPA, and now plays in the newly formed PWHL between her national hockey commitments. I asked Sarah about her thoughts on women's professional hockey, and what is really needed in order to make WoHo succeed in the professional hockey landscape of today. For Sarah, who holds a bachelor's degree in business from the University of Wisconsin–Madison, prior to the PWHL the leagues lacked the level of business savvy that players had become privy to while playing college hockey or on a national team.

"The gap between being an amateur hockey player and being a national player . . . that's really what needs to change," Sarah told me. "The biggest thing I think for us is just the professionalism, when we're talking about women's hockey. I went to the University of Wisconsin, and we were treated like professional athletes. The way we travelled, what we got, how business was run, how day-to-day operations were run; we were professional hockey players. When we're with Hockey Canada, we are treated as professional hockey players. Currently, that professionalism is lacking in that in-between stage; that's the real problem. It's not necessarily the money per se, because there are players being paid very well now to play professional [PHF] hockey. But it is that element of professionalism that is really, really missing. There are some players who are getting paid incredibly like Mikyla [Grant-Mentis], but not everybody's getting paid as much as she is. Even what she's making, compared to other professional women's leagues and men's professional leagues, is not where it needs to be. We just need that professionalism to really up the ante. When I look at women's professional hockey in the way that it's regarded, it's not afforded the same respect . . . as other women's professional leagues. Even when people look at me, and they talk about me playing hockey, it's still not the same as when people talk with somebody playing in the WNBA. Especially in Canada, which is shocking, because we have zero of those teams. Zero of these teams, and hockey is our national sport."

"As we move forward, I think it's a problem when we have professional hockey teams playing in community arenas. Yes, you're walking in as a minor hockey player on a Tuesday night, and a professional women's hockey team is warming up in the lobby. That's not a good look. So it's these little things that add up to people not taking women's professional hockey seriously. I think those little things are eventually going to create big change."

At the time of our conversation, the PWHL would not debut its six teams—three in Canada and three in the United States—for another two years. While it's too early to say whether all of Sarah's goals have been met, the new league seems to be committed to growth and sustainability. That's a promising start.

For a player like Sarah Nurse, who has had a thriving hockey career, it is possible to look back and feel satisfaction in her accomplishments. As one of the superstars of the newly formed PWHL, she seems to be in a place that allows her to look at her future in hockey spaces differently than any other Black woman who has played professional hockey. She can see the disparities but she has also had a successful career that is leading to even more innovation and "firsts."

"If I did not play hockey ever again," Sarah admitted when we spoke, "I think that I would be very at peace with that. When I was young, I wanted to play for Team Canada. Check. I wanted to go to the Olympics. Check. I wanted to win a gold medal. Check! Right? For me, I just feel like that is a hockey career that I've always wanted to have. I think I would feel very at peace if the next chapter was ready to happen."

While the PWHL as the newest iteration of WoHo is exciting for fans and players alike, it is still very much a white woman's game. Diversity of thought comes with actual diversity, and in WoHo spaces, just like in the rest of hockey, the majority of folks involved in growing the game are white. This means that those of us who are non-white advocates for WoHo still have to fight for our voices to be heard and our intersections to be acknowledged and valued. There are powerful ways in which white women can be advocates for marginalized folks, but it often involves stepping aside and letting others lead, which doesn't really *feel* like girlbossing, amirite?!

A great example of intersectional allyship was when, in 2020, Liz Knox, professional women's hockey player, voluntarily stepped down from her position on the PWHPA board to make room for Sarah Nurse. In an article by Emily Kaplan of ESPN, Sarah was quoted as saying about the situation: "It was a pretty selfless act of allyship. There was a lack of diverse representation, and for her to recognize that is a showcase of allyship. We talk about hiring Black people, hiring Indigenous people, but few people recognize that [and] then walk the walk. Liz is a leader by example."

Really, subverting white supremacy and the patriarchy comes down to doing what you can in the spaces you occupy. If I've said it once, I've said it a thousand times: we can only do what we can do. And for Liz, what she had in her power to do was step aside and let a Black woman lead. Unfortunately, capitalism, patriarchy, and white supremacy place so much value on gaining and maintaining power that equity can feel painful, even discriminatory. The toxicity of white feminism lies in a fear of losing control that leads certain white women to perpetuate harmful practices in order to keep some of it. By leveraging whiteness against Black women, white feminism aligns itself with white supremacy in order to maintain a semblance of power. A tale as old as time! In the nineteenth century, Elizabeth Cady Stanton and Susan B. Anthony lobbied against Black voting rights and supported white women gaining the right to vote instead. Rather than view the interests of race and gender as similarly affected by white supremacy, white feminists would rather double down on their anti-Blackness in order to maintain proximity to whiteness and the power inherent there. While this tactic can seem beneficial in the moment, it reveals an insidious lack of solidarity, a lack of awareness, and, ultimately, a self-centred view of community.

In communities that share responsibilities and burdens, we also share authority, but in white supremacist patriarchal societies, communal leadership isn't true power. White supremacy will tell us that true power is unquestionable, unwavering, undying, and unmoved. Horizontal power structures led by women who share the burdens and blessings of leadership, and are able to build successful spaces within our American capitalist society, are really few and far between. Although I am trying to build BGHC to be such a space, it isn't profitable and we are often overlooked, undervalued, copied, or ignored because we do not function at the same frequency as so many other nonprofits, even Black-led ones. It is a dynamic that I struggle with constantly—this need to build, work, and subvert inside a system that is designed to chew me up and spit me out. And with this duality comes a dual experience in feminist spaces. While I want to support all women, not all women support me. How do I deal with that? How would you?

Another example of intersectional allyship was the 2022 Black History Month capsule art project organized by the

Metropolitan Riveters alongside Black Girl Hockey Club. The image of Rosie the Riveter (red lips, bandana in the hair, flexed arm) is very much blazed onto the American consciousness, and represents a kind of stoic, American, proud version of womanhood during the Second World War. Rosie is strong; she works hard; she is proud; she is selfless; she is white. Well, many of the women working in the factories while the men were away at war were actually Black, but unfortunately American history erases that narrative, as well as the fact that Rosie and her white sisters were forced out of those jobs when the men returned. This, in fact, prompted (white) feminist activists to burn bras, lobby for abortion rights, and break into the boardrooms of the patriarchy, girlbossing their way to the glass ceiling enforced by patriarchal white supremacy.

But I digress.

What the PHF's Metropolitan Riveters wanted to do was honour the contributions of Black women to American history with a collection featuring a Black Rosie on branded Riveters merchandise, including a jersey to be worn at least once on the ice. Ultimately, the partnership became an exercise in creating a systemic level of change within an organization run by white women, and recognizing the ways in which white feminism works for and against intersectional feminism. A portion of the sales of all capsule merch came back to BGHC— which sent a powerful message to the WoHo community about accountability and cold hard cash. Working directly on the capsule with the Riveters gave Jordan Dabney, the BGHC artist and Black Rosie designer, a boost of confidence and visibility in hockey spaces—a wonderful thing to see happen for a young Black artist and hockey fan.

The Riveters also hired Jasmine Baker to do their PR that season—an amazing move that gave me the chance to work closely with another queer Black woman in hockey who was getting paid to be there. Jasmine worked for months planning a BGHC takeover at the Metropolitan Riveters' arena in New Jersey at the end of February 2022. While I unfortunately ended up missing the event because I caught COVID-19 a few days before my flight, a good group got together to enjoy the festivities and the fruits of all the hard work.

The capsule collection was a success, the fans and the media loved it, and even the men's hockey world took notice of the Black Rosie phenomenon. In my opinion, the project was a WoHo accomplishment that showed how integral Black folks are to women's hockey. But the Riveters' Black Rosie project cannot be discussed without also mentioning Erica Ayala and her contributions to the concept.

After years of conversation with the Riveters about the concept of a Black Rosie capsule collection, but no action to move it forward, Erica had commissioned Jo Dabney to create an original piece for use as Erica's media company logo. Black Rosie Media was born before the Riveters' version of Black Rosie was created, but at the time of the capsule launch Erica's original idea was lost in the media frenzy over the collection. Then, only a few weeks after the launch, the Riveters leadership collapsed with the hiring of Digit Murphy as team president. Digit was coming from the PHF's Toronto Six, and was a popular WoHo coach with a troubling history of working with transphobic leadership that she has since denounced with a (not great) apology to trans communities. BGHC had been working closely with Riveters general manager Anya Packer, who was our main point of contact during her year-long tenure—which was great, at first. Not so great after Anya, Jasmine, and others left the organization, and I realized BGHC had no agreements in writing, only emails and verbal conversations, and no one who had quit was really checking their emails anymore. It wasn't easy to figure out, but to their credit, Digit, Jasmine, and Anya did what they could to make sure BGHC got paid quickly and efficiently.

The most disappointing part of the project was that an active partnership seemed to end with the change of leadership. BGHC and the audience we represent just stopped being a priority. This isn't a criticism of the Rivs, however. The team, their staff, and folks like Anya did more than any other PHF team to actively engage with Black women in hockey spaces, and I am proud of our partnership. I am proud of all the partnerships that have been cultivated with hockey organizations led by non-Black folks, particularly other women who want to effect a culture shift within ice hockey. I guess what gets to me is the way that non-Black women—let's be real, white women—can just walk away from intersectional issues that do not directly concern them. They can cut themselves off from interacting with social issues surrounding marginalized folks, and instead focus on their families, or writing a book, or working from home while focusing on their families and writing a book and bam! All of a sudden their Instagram feed is full of only other white people and you wonder if you might have been their only Black friend.

It confuses me when the women I sit next to on panels or who reach out to discuss anti-racism don't engage socially with BIPOC folks. It seems impossible to me that in the year of our Lord 2024, there are white people who only talk to or hang out with other white people. The demographics of the world are such that a move like that has to be intentional, right? I mean, gerrymandering and neighbourhood segregation aside, the internet exists and we all have access to so much information and so many different types of people. If white women are in friend groups, church groups, school groups, book clubs, country clubs, and hockey clubs with only other white women, I mean, that has got to be on purpose, right?

This intentional segregation makes me question which of my white women colleagues will continue to lift up anti-racist POVs in the long term, and continue to support me and the work that I do even when the lights, cameras, and accolades are gone. I am leery of anyone who would rather be blissfully ignorant than painfully aware. James Baldwin once said, "Ignorance, allied with power, is the most ferocious enemy justice can have." White supremacy offers power to white women, if only they remain ignorant—whether wilfully or accidentally—of the unique experiences of other marginalized people. The intoxication of the authority offered by white supremacy can only be counterbalanced by authentic connections to communities of colour, queer communities, and disabled communities.

White feminism makes it impossible to authentically engage with intersectionality because the ideology of white feminism is not inclusive. According to Koa Beck, journalist and author of the book *White Feminism*, the ideology and strategy of white feminism "focuses more on individual accumulation, capital and individuality." I'm not one to preach the humanization of marginalized folks to white people; it isn't my burden to prove my humanity to anyone. But white feminism fights against acknowledging my intersections, instead leaning into a girlboss version of the patriarchal capitalism that got us here in the first place—and by "here," I mean on the other side of statewide abortion bans, book bans in schools, and many, many children dead at the hands of white supremacists and their AR-15s. These are feminist problems just as much as the wage gap, medical racism, and trans-exclusionary laws are, and if I am in a room with the ability to use my voice and white people are listening? I'm going to speak up against this toxicity, because maybe no one else will.

In April 2023, at the invitation of Mary-Kay Messier, Vice President of Global Marketing for Bauer Hockey and BGHC super-fan, I travelled to Toronto to speak on the "Accelerate Women's Hockey" panel alongside women from Bauer Hockey, Stathletes, Canada's Sports Network (TSN), Future of Hockey Lab, and Women's Para Hockey of Canada. Representing BGHC, I was the only person of colour speaking, with Tekeyah Singh of TSN added a few days before the event as our panel moderator. In preparation for what would be an event full of hockey bigwigs at the freakin' Hockey Hall of Fame, the panellists met on Zoom a few times to develop topics, questions, and a general direction for the conversation. Throughout the process, I struggled to find my place in the group, as I continuously felt the need to bring the conversation back to the intersections of Black women and how they make for a unique experience in hockey spaces. The panellists were all powerhouses in hockey: CEOs, executive directors, founders; straight, white, able-bodied, cisgender women in hockey. And me! I know I'm a founder and an executive director and a powerhouse, I'm not discounting that, but the fact that I was the only woman of colour meant that I had to offer a wide range of intersectional perspectives not otherwise present. I spent a lot of my time wondering if I was in the right place, but ultimately decided I had to bring my voice to the conversation. If not me, then who? The audience at this event promised to represent some of the biggest international hockey organizations, and here was my chance to have their ears for a few sweet minutes and curate a powerful conversation with the other panellists that could potentially change the way those listening and the organizations they represented engaged with hockey. At least that's the way I like to go into these types of conversations: we're changing the world here! But also, gently, right?

The pressure to represent Black culture in a palatable way to white folks is a real challenge for Black women. We are forced to balance our Blackness, our womanness, perhaps our queerness or disabilities, in a way that allows white folks, particularly white women, to continue to feel good about themselves. We can talk about racism in a general way, but let's not bring it too close to home, or else we might not be invited back to speak at the conference, submit to the journal, or get that promotion we deserve. Shireen Ahmed said "white feminism" on a panel one time and someone started crying! White Woman Tears are no joke!

When I became frustrated with myself and a little nervous to say my piece ahead of the Bauer panel, I reached out to a friend (Shireen) to discuss the real challenges of speaking for Black women (in her case, Muslim women) in white-women-led spaces. It isn't easy to be the one constantly reminding white women that the experiences of Black women (and Muslim women) are different, that in addition to sexism and misogyny we also face racism, and that we are unable to separate our Blackness (Muslimah) from our womanhood, and nor should we be expected to. I often feel guilty bringing up my Blackness around white folks. *Here comes Renee, reminding white people they're white, again.*

Ultimately, it isn't my job to solve racism or remind others of my intersectional identity, my experiences, and where society has failed me and others who look like me. Still, as a Black woman occupying a very white space, I set personal expectations and values that I feel bound to uphold. People who know me recognize that I am my own worst critic. And trust me, I understand that it can be tedious to have to think or talk about race, gender, sexuality, disability, age, and other intersections *all the time*. I am not saying this constant vigil against racism isn't exhausting. It really, really is. But Black women don't have the luxury of ignorance. Being woke and aware of the Black experience in America and across the world has caused me to question relationships, end friendships, and look at family members differently. It has forced me to evaluate my own privilege, my authenticity, and my sanity as the world continues to turn around us and society is *clearly* falling apart.

The day after the Bauer panel, the panellists and the organizations we represented were invited to see Canada play Sweden at the IIHF Women's World Championship quarterfinal game. Together, we got the chance to witness the true professionalism of national women's hockey; and, of course, a Sarah Nurse overtime goal to win the game for Canada. The crowd was fairly homogenous, with the BGHC crew making up the majority of melanated faces in the crowd, but the vibes were immaculate. It felt like magic—watching the Olympic gold medal–winning Canadian women's team skating for a sea of fans decked out in red and white, with the sold-out arena thrumming with energy. And there was something even more special about seeing Sarah Nurse score the OT game-winning goal to advance the team to the semifinals in front of a bunch of little Black girl hockey players and their families. It's in those moments that I am reminded of why I stay on message, why I continue to put myself out there as the only one, the first one, the loudest in the room. Because if I don't, and if *we* don't stand up for ourselves and for the little Black girls who come through those doors after us, who will? Who will advocate for us if *not* us?

What feminism steeped in white supremacy teaches young girls is that the intersections that make us different are less important than the fact that we are women. This is why TERF-ism, or trans-exclusionary radical feminism, is so dangerous and alluring to white women. *Uncover a* TERF *and you will uncover a racist* is the old internet adage. While fighting against the inclusion of trans women in their rigid definition of gender, TERFs are really arguing against the experience of individuals in favour of institutional norms set up by white supremacy, which keeps whiteness and femininity supreme and untouchable. This just reinforces the patriarchy and white supremacy, fam. Gender, sexuality, race—these are social constructs created to divide us and build false walls around us, so that we don't feel empathy for our fellow human beings. White feminists clutch their pearls at what "those people" are doing to "our country," and reinforce exclusionary tactics and politics that leave this shared land raped, pillaged, and colonized—to the detriment of all.

Ultimately, Black women cannot girlboss our way to the top of anything. Those tactics do not work for us, they are not meant for us, and they will never, ever benefit us the way we want them to. So we have to do things differently, and we do. We engage in community care, and build spaces for other Black girls, and we step up for marginalized communities that are not our own, because our collective liberation is more important than individual gain, and the only strategy that will successfully defeat white supremacy. White feminism will never help us, only harm us. And to my non-Black sisters, please, recognize these toxic, exclusionary tactics for what they are, and use your privilege to build up communities instead of breaking them down.

CHANGING THE WORLD IS ALWAYS BETTER WITH FRIENDS

For people of colour, women, LGBTQ people, and disabled folks, hockey can feel demoralizing, and at times frustratingly unwelcoming. When it gets difficult, we head to the proverbial group chat, where we can share our fears alongside our favourite memes to lighten the burdens of the day. This is the core of a community that thrives online, and a support system that helps shape sports activism. But how does one even get *into* a group chat? The process is different for everyone, but I will be your guide, faithful reader, as we explore the importance of online community spaces and how you TOO can score an invite to the cool kids' GC.

First of all, finding online community begins with engaging folks who like and comment under the same posts as you—but avoid the trolls and stick to positive engagements, unless you're looking for an argument. (If that's the case, do you, boo!) A good place to start is sending your favourite fandom memes or posts to the cool, nice nerds who use the same hashtags as you. Not those corporate hashtags that the institutions use, but the ones developed by folks you vibe with. The hope is that you will get invited to an already functioning group chat—with the permission of the others in the GC, of course. This consensus is not always necessary, but good GC etiquette considers it rude to invite someone to a smooth-running chat space without checking with the main members.

It should be noted that new members may not quite fit in at first. Hopping into a GC with a group of long-time fandom friends can feel like a trial by fire, because one must either engage and quickly make friends, or get lost in a sea of inside jokes and misunderstood references. But it is possible to develop deep relationships in these long-term group chats, which can move from platform to platform depending on how long the shared interests last. For those of us who are *older*, there was LiveJournal and AOL chat; nowadays, elders like myself might keep the chat to Slack (work friends), Twitter (active fandom friends), or WhatsApp (international fandom friends).

My longest-running GC started in October 2014 as a WhatsApp group dedicated to discussing season ten of the CW show *Supernatural*, and was set up by a person who isn't even in the group anymore. Instead of deleting us, she handed over the torch and shared administrative duties so that we wouldn't lose our archives. That's a true-blue GC friend right there. Now, we all know that *Supernatural* ended in 2020, and some of this group (not I) stopped watching the show years before the finale even aired, so this GC mainly sends links to tweets about what our favourite *Supernatural* actors are doing now and pictures of our pets and/or kids. There is something comforting about the widget for this WhatsApp group staying the same on my cellphone home screen, even as I get new devices and the years pass us by. We have seen each other through not only the end of our favourite TV show, but real-life marriages and divorces, births and birthdays—and, as we grow older, the deaths of loved ones. When I told the girls that I wanted to write about our group chat in this book, they were overwhelmingly supportive. I then asked them if I could write about us and about Holli, one of the people in our fandom chat, who passed away on July 22, 2021, just a few months after our Christmas video chat—a moment Holli had insisted we all make time for, regardless of time zones. Holli used to send me links to her favourite transformative (fanfic) works, she always commented on my Instagram pictures, and she had two gorgeous babies while texting the GC updates the entire time!

Holli was our resident expert on Random Acts, the nonprofit organization founded by *Supernatural* actor Misha Collins in 2010. She began working with Random Acts in 2018, and remained a big part of the organization until she died. Since I joined the GC in 2014, members all over the world, from New Zealand to Idaho, have gotten together in person to go to conventions, have dinner, and enjoy international fandom adventures—often in the name of *Supernatural*, but also just as friends. I never got to meet Holli in person, but she sometimes sent me Christmas cards. We all miss her in the chat and talk about her often.

I was invited into this group soon after its inception, so I imagine there was some sort of consensus that my personality would fit into this particular space. You notice I didn't give this group a name, and that's because since 2015 it's been this butt emoticon: (_|_). I'm truly honoured I made the cut! I anticipate that those of us who are left in this group will continue to send thirst tweets and fic recs to one another until we too pass away, and I know that's what Holli would have wanted.

If there isn't an already-formed GC that allows you to join its ranks, another option is to find a group of like-minded friends and collectively form a group chat around a particular interest. This is how Black Girl Hockey Club came about, tangentially. While engaging with fellow hockey fans on social media, I asked half a dozen Black women I'd met on Hockey Twitter if they wanted to start a group chat. We mutually agreed, and all hopped into the group with varying levels of friendship existing between us. I actually didn't get too involved in the day-to-day conversation in this particular group, but when it came to naming this chat, I took the initiative and jokingly called us "BGHC" or "Black Girl Hockey Club," although I'm not sure anyone but me got the joke.

While the idea for BGHC started as a Twitter chat, not many of the original Twitter group members were actually involved in the development of Black Girl Hockey Club as an organization, except for two—who continue to show up to support the organized endeavour, joined me at our first-ever meet-up in Washington, D.C., back in December 2018, and volunteered behind the scenes to help get BGHC off the ground. Since then, the BGHC Twitter group has dissolved, with the original members scattering across hockey social media. I'm not even sure who else was in that OG group, to be honest, but I won't soon forget the support from these women and how they helped me build my BGHC dream simply by being my mutuals.

Speaking of mutuals: the last tip I have for you, dear reader, is to get to know the mutual friends that you share with your followers. This helps grow your circles and can lead to collaborations and expanding your fandom horizons. I discovered hockey because so many of my *Supernatural* fandom friends followed and shared the progress of a hockey webcomic called *Check, Please!* by a Black woman writer called Ngozi. I kept seeing adorable fan art of hockey boys and pie on my Tumblr feed, and I got curious! My good friend San Diego Liz (I call her that even though she's from Wisconsin, because pre-pandemic we used to meet at San Diego Comic-Con every summer) is a sports fan, and I reached out to her via WhatsApp and asked if she knew anything about hockey. She shared some fic recs and YouTube links, and told me all about Tyler Seguin, the Dallas Stars hockey player who has enticed many newbies with his himbo grin and goal-scoring ability—respectfully. Through SD Liz, I discovered Stars Twitter, followed some of her Stars fan friends, and began engaging with the #GoStars hashtag alongside other women on game days and during big team events.

As someone who came to the game of hockey later in life, I had the resources to develop this new hobby in a way I wouldn't have had even ten years before. I was able to engage online, purchase the NHL television package, pay for game tickets, buy team gear, and travel. Not everyone has that privilege. Which is why the most important part of developing a hockey obsession for me was to find people to talk to about where I fit into the sport and where I did not.

It was on Stars Twitter that I found my first group of hockey-fan friends. We gathered our mutuals and made a WhatsApp group chat we lovingly called the "Sin Bin." It still exists, years later, and functions in much the same way that my *Supernatural* chat does. Not all of us are quite as into hockey as we used to be, but we use the space to give life updates, send the most dramatic of hockey news, and share the occasional Tyler Seguin meme. As with the (_|_) GC, members communicate across various mediums and from various places, from California to the U.K. And the Sin Bin girlies have developed friendships outside of hockey, outside of the group environment, and literally *outside*. It's been lovely to meet so many new people through a shared interest via social media, and it's a nice reminder that the internet doesn't always have to be an awful place.

Within fandom spaces, the group chat can feel like an essential part of survival. It is a place where folks who love or hate (or a little bit of both) a team, TV show, film, band, or piece of (sub)cultural art can come together to discuss and interact with those who share similar interests or viewpoints. From the "pens-fans-crying-space" that the BGHC volunteers have on Slack (yes, I started it for the many Penguins fans who volunteer for my non-profit, and yes, we cry about Sidney Crosby ~~sometimes~~ often) to the butt-emoticon *Supernatural* WhatsApp group I've been in for almost a decade, there is a GC for everything. Particularly in sports, it is imperative that like-minded peers who have been marginalized by systems of oppression have an outlet to privately share the insights, the horrors, and the joys of working within these institutions. For Black women, LGBTQ folks, and people of colour who work and play in these spaces, as well as our co-conspirators in our anti-racism efforts, there is an unspoken agreement to amplify and lift one another up, and this takes on a tangible shape in fan-led movements like Black Girl Hockey Club, because that is one thing we all have in common: we are fans—of sports, of hockey, of each other—and we act accordingly. We consult with one another on projects, we get together for hockey games, we share our joys, and we commiserate together when things get rough in the hockey world. If you're doing it right, you might just make some lifelong friends along the way.

I've met a lot of amazing people on the internet, but one of the most important relationships I've developed online is with award-winning journalist Shireen Ahmed. Shireen is an independent contributor for the CBC and a podcast host, and in the past few years she has become one of my best friends. Back in 2018, as I began to navigate sports advocacy and look for women with similar interests and attitudes on social media, I found the precision and clarity of Shireen's writing on sports to be a balm in a space that needed more diversity of thought as well as *actual* diversity. When she invited me to be a guest on her podcast, *Burn It All Down*, during Black History Month in February 2019, I accepted because I was a fan of her writing and saw an opportunity to connect my burgeoning endeavours with BGHC to the larger social justice movement in sports.

Shireen's values are right there in her work, and she isn't shy about penning articles on everything from trans rights for athletes to sexual assault in national sports team systems. As a hijab-wearing, Canadian-born woman of Pakistani heritage who uses her platform to fight against injustices in and around sports, Shireen is a pillar of her local sports and local Muslim communities. I got to experience her impact on these communities first-hand when Black Girl Hockey Club visited Toronto in April 2022 and I spent a week as a guest in Shireen's home during the holy month of Ramadan. While hockey isn't her first love (that would be soccer), the sport has been part of her life since she started playing at the age of five. As Shireen makes sure to tell everyone when she talks about hockey, her mother, Dr. Tahira Ahmed, is a diehard Montreal Canadiens fan, and has been ever since the Ahmeds moved to Ottawa from Pakistan in 1972. In order to integrate into the local community, they did what many immigrant families who move to Canada do—they got involved in hockey.

"Now that I think about it, my mother put us in this league so that we would wear Habs jerseys!" Shireen exclaimed during our single recorded interview for this book, back in May 2021. It's twice as long as any of my other interviews, but that's because we took the first hour to gossip, catch up, and laugh together. When Shireen first reached out to me in 2019 to be a guest on *Burn It All Down*, I had no expectations and certainly no idea that we would develop a deep, abiding friendship, especially because we live on opposite sides of North America, in different countries. We made plans to meet in person back in April 2020, but the pandemic hit, and the conference she was meant to attend in Los Angeles was cancelled due to alarming numbers of COVID deaths and city-wide restrictions. We ended up spending three years chatting online, via various platforms, before meeting for the first time in Boston in January 2022, for the Bruins' Willie O'Ree jersey retirement at TD Garden and the inaugural Carnegie Initiative Summit. Shireen consulted with Bryant McBride, co-founder of the Carnegie Initiative, during the planning process, and was asked to moderate a panel on diversity in media for the conference portion of the event. The summit was great—full of networking and fundraising opportunities, as well as big names in sports and advocacy. I even got to enjoy a Bruins game, and watched the O'Ree jersey raised to the rafters as a guest in Kim Davis's suite. But the best part of the entire two-day affair was undoubtedly me and Shireen, hanging out for forty-eight hours straight; eating, laughing, and vibing, just like we had been doing together online for the past three years.

In order to build meaningful relationships, we must come together as a community for a common cause or purpose. Although Shireen and I come from different backgrounds, religions, and parts of the world, we have found a rich commonality in our world views, highlighted through our work in sports. We have mutual values and goals, and we run in the same circles. It was meant to be! Along with Shireen and seven others, I belong to a private group chat that is called "The Pronoun Gang," because all the members have pronouns in our bios, which means there is an entire subsection of the internet that hates us. This is a community of educators, advocates, and workers who represent various marginalized groups in hockey, and who may or may not be fairly well-known in some hockey spaces. But just because we are exclusive doesn't mean we don't care about what goes on in the world around us! It's quite the opposite, actually. With hockey facing a slew of racist incidents in the past few years, from thirteen-year-old Divyne Apollon II being called the N-word on the ice in December 2018—the same month BGHC had our first meet-up—to Nazem Kadri being racially abused on social media during his successful 2022 Stanley Cup run with the Colorado Avalanche, it seems there is always something shitty going down in hockey. The Pronoun Gang GC is where I go when there is a niche issue that only marginalized hockey fans who work in hockey will understand. We love the game so much—even though there aren't so many folks who look like us, even though we can sometimes be tokenized in this space, even though hockey as a culture tells us time and time again that we are not actually welcome or that we are an afterthought. We keep coming back, making space, doing the work, and building community. We love the game even when the game doesn't love us back.

A group chat is not out-of-the-ordinary for folks who work in sports, and our GC is populated by folks from all over—across leagues, organizations, systems, and nations. We network. We talk about what teams, leagues, players, and executives we enjoy working with and those we don't—off the record, of course. We discuss how to mentor other marginalized folks with intentionality, in order to infiltrate all aspects of hockey, including the C-suites. Each one of us, however large or small our role in sports may be, is committed to making room in hockey for Black women. We send each other gift baskets and vouchers for spa days when the trauma of bending to the will of racist institutions gets to be too much.

When people talk about the power of cancel culture, what they're really talking about is marginalized folks taking back the only power we have—which is the power to spend our money, consume, and engage with entertainment, organizations, and individuals that align with our personal values. When it seems the vast majority of sports culture doesn't appreciate our perspectives or our pushing for change, we lift one another up with our community *within* the community. The Pronoun Gang group chat provides yet another example of how successful anti-racist movements uplift one another by utilizing empathy, clear communication, and trust.

"It's not to say that Black Girl Hockey Club has solved racism," Shireen joked in our interview. "That's not what's happening here, but there's a tangible shift and there's the holding of joy. That doesn't happen enough. And it's how there's space for that here. That's why I love when we're in the BGHC volunteer Slack chat. We're talking about work stuff and someone will say, *Oh, but this game,* and then we'll banter about hockey, which I think is really important. Isn't that the root of it? We're connected by this sport, right?

"People think of intersectionality as a negative space. And I don't think they realize that in the intersections that exist—because that's where we exist—there is joy. And they haven't learned that yet. We wouldn't be doing this if it wasn't for the joy we felt in these spaces. Like ultimately, I do love hockey. I think the game is fabulous. I love watching it. I love feeling it. One of my bucket list items is to go to a Black Girl Hockey Club meet-up in a stadium. I'll even go to a Pens game for you, Renee." Which is a huge admission from a lifelong Habs fan who carries an unholy grudge against Nova Scotian hockey hero Sidney Crosby. Shireen, you really *do* love me!

In one of her shorter essays, Audre Lorde explicitly discusses an NYU conference she attended in 1979, at which she was one of two Black women invited to take part in an event commemorating the thirtieth anniversary of Simone de Beauvoir's *The Second Sex*. Her experience was not a good one, and the piece details the ways Lorde felt tokenized, isolated, and dismissed. The criticism is right there in the essay title, "The

Master's Tools Will Never Dismantle the Master's House." But there is no mistaking Lorde's message: acknowledging our differences as well as our commonalities will strengthen the movement toward global liberation. Sharing in and learning from the struggles of others will enable us to create lasting change. We must treat people better and do things differently than they have always been done, especially within our social groups, community-based non-profits, and employee inclusion committees, or we will fail and we will deserve it. In order to hold folks accountable, we must start with ourselves, our communities—and, of course, the group chat.

For those who work in spaces that have not historically been meant for them, the group chat becomes a valuable form of not only communication but community and wellness. Sarah Nurse is a busy woman—she manages much of her own marketing, she excels at brand endorsements and takes paid speaking gigs all over the world, plus she trains on and off the ice all year long.

As a high-level athlete, Sarah has spent much of her life under a spotlight and knows a great deal about pressure as well as being the "only one." She also recognizes the importance of building and maintaining support systems in order to not only thrive but develop ideas and facilitate change. "I've never actually met Blake Bolden, right? But we talk all the time," she tells me. "Like every time she sees me somewhere, every time I see her somewhere, like, we're chatting when we check in on each other. We make sure everything's okay. *How are you feeling this weekend? Have a great weekend? Take your rest, right?* Because I see her out in L.A., doing absolutely everything. And I'm like, *Honey, you need a vacation.*

Right? Yeah. So it's been kind of cool, because I've been able to talk to Blake and Kelsey [Koelzer] and Saroya [Tinker], and just kind of build this sense of community because we all have similar but different experiences. We've all had the similar experience where we've been the only ones, so being able to check in on each other, it's probably been the best thing that's come out of all of this."

In her tenure as a hockey player, Sarah has never experienced an organization that centres Black women quite the way that BGHC does. The concept inspired her, and early in the pandemic she joined our first-ever virtual meet-up to just hang out with other Black girl hockey fans. She also posted a picture of herself in a BGHC hoodie on her personal Instagram grid, exposing our organization to her 53,000 followers at a time when we were just starting out.

"When we're talking about Black Girl Hockey Club, it's really just vital. You need a support system, you need some sort of community, wherever you are. And so within the hockey world, we have different places where we feel welcome, and okay, and know that there's like a 'no judgment zone' where you can say what you want to say, where you can get out what you need to get out. And so having that community within the hockey world is important, really, for mental health and your emotions, and really everything. Because that's what you need in any industry in the world that you're in," Sarah says—and she's not wrong.

For those of us who are part of marginalized communities, when we engage in professional sports, we are stepping into a world in which we are not meant to have any power, in which there is little to no diversity or representation, and in which the onus is unjustly placed on us to educate our oppressors about our own humanity. For someone outside of the traditional demographic, working in hockey can feel isolating, and the high mental toll that discrimination takes is taxing. Having a space to connect with people who have similar experiences as you—well, that feeling is priceless. It feels like coming home.

When Sarah accepted our invitation to be part of the "Brilliant Blackness of Women in Hockey" panel in Toronto, it was the first time she had been in a room with so many Black folks to discuss hockey. On most days, she speaks with white folks about hockey. At those events, there are no practical conversations about how to fit braids under a hockey helmet or even what music gets played in a locker room of 99 per cent white folks and one Black player, let alone deep discussions about social justice. If racial issues are mentioned at all, the focus is often on trauma.

Many times, Black folks in hockey are not only isolated, we are tokenized, with some of our most painful moments put on display. So many of us have had our negative experiences centred by non-marginalized folks, because discrimination-based trauma and abuse are easier to understand than the microaggressions that whittle away at self-confidence and self-worth and that many non-Black folks actively participate in. For young Black girl hockey players, the sport can feel especially isolating. For many of the BGHC scholarship girls it's much like it was for Sarah growing up—they are the only Black person on their team or even in their league. Most of them have never played against another Black player. Imagine that! Loving a sport, participating in it, and working hard to make it onto a team, and never once seeing a person on the ice who looked

Renee, Henry (dad), Becky (mom), and Sarah (sister) pose for a family picture in Corvallis, Oregon, June 1982.

Blake Bolden, Lauryn Fray (niece), and Lola Hess (daughter) attend the first PWHPA showcase event in Los Angeles, December 2022.

Renee brandishing her sign at Evgeni Malkin during warm-ups at her very first Penguins home game, Pittsburgh, February 2020.

Renee at her second Penguins home game of the week enjoying community with BGHC for her birthday, Pittsburgh, October 2022.

Delvina Morrow, Tracey McCants Lewis, and Renee are all smiles after a successful BHM event with the Penguins, February 2023.

Ashley Craig, Renee, Brian Burke, and Teresa Shine pose together at the Pittsburgh Penguins Black Hockey History Game, Pittsburgh, February 2023.

Taj-Aura Hood, Renee, P.O. Joseph, and
Teresa Shine enjoy a laugh together post-game,
February 2023.

Renee enjoying the Dallas Stars and her very first hockey game, Anaheim, January 2016.

Samantha Shipka (sister), Corinne Douglas, Nora Douglas, Kelsey Koelzer, Kristine Koelzer, and Renee enjoy brunch before the very first Black Girl Hockey Club meet-up with the Washington Capitals in DC, December 2018.

Renee meets Willie O'Ree for the first time after friends of the burgeoning BGHC crowdfunded for her to attend an award ceremony for him at the Canadian Embassy, Washington, DC, February 2019.

Renee seeing her *New York Times* profile on paper for the first time, Riverside, CA, September 2020.

Coach Mike and Lincoln Brown at Culver Academy Academies for Parents' Weekend, Culver, IN, October 2022.

BGHC Board of Directors Annual Meet & Greet Retreat, Las Vegas, August 2023.

Renee, Shireen Ahmed, Sarah Nurse, Saroya Tinker, Dayton O'Donoghue, and Raegan Subban at MLSE LaunchPad for the "BGHC Toronto Takeover" and the panel event "The Brilliant Blackness of Women in Hockey," April 2022.

Paikea Baylis, Dr. Courtney Szto, Shireen Ahmed, Sarah Nurse, Fatou Bah, Dayton O'Donoghue, and Raegan Subban at MLSE Launchpad, April 2022.

Renee with Sarah Nurse's gold medal, April 2022.

Renee, Angela James, Taylor Green, Saroya Tinker, Bernice Carnegie, Amrit Gill, and Raegan Subban at e11even Restaurant for the Maple Leafs–hosted luncheon "Celebrating Black Women in Hockey" in Toronto, April 2022.

Renee and Saroya Tinker at the BGHC Canada launch event in Toronto, Ontario, November 2022.

BGHC goes to our first Maple Leafs game in Toronto, April 2022.

Tekeyah Singh, Renee, Amy Walsh, Meghan Chayka, and Tara Chisholm speaking at a panel event hosted by Bauer Hockey held at the Hockey Hall of Fame in Toronto, April 2023.

Renee, Paikea Baylis, Gem Winter, Angela James, Makayla Sheppard, and Emerson Henry at the Carnegie Initiative Summit in Toronto, January 2024.

like you? Who shared a similar cultural background? It's a loneliness and forced assimilation that so many marginalized folks understand, and Black women in particular sit at a very unique intersection. We have to field questions on our hair, our music, our clothes, our religion, our gender, our sexuality, our disabilities, our people. Alone. It's exhausting. It's why Black communities scoff at ice hockey and tell each other: *Black people don't do hockey.* It's why so many Black parents opt out of hockey for their kids. It's why there is low retention in the sport for Black boys and girls. They "Learn to Play," and then what? How does hockey, as an institution, create generational fans in Black communities?

These are the topics that we discussed in Toronto, as a community, with Sarah and the other panellists. They are also the things the BGHC scholarship girls talk about in their own team chat, hosted by mentor Saroya Tinker. For leaders like Saroya, a group chat is imperative to team development. Giving these young women a space to be themselves, to be Black girl hockey players, can potentially change the game for them.

"I wanted to inspire other Black girls to make it to where I've made it and not feel alienated, and find a new purpose for playing, really," says Saroya. "Putting the information out there for them, networking and things like that."

As in every field, in hockey, networking is not only valuable, but necessary, particularly for marginalized communities. Currently, the BGHC Canada Slack group has forty-six members. From hockey-playing BGHC scholarship winners and their parents to board members and Saroya Tinker herself, the members range widely in age as well as in their relationship to the sport. These are lifelong connections born in a very unique, Black woman-led hockey space. "I've made it for everyone now rather than just those girls, but there's also girls that are reporters, or are involved in the hockey community in another sense that want to join. I think that's important for not only my girls that are being recruited, but for the ones that just need a community and people to talk to that love the same thing that they love.

"Most of my involvement is with my older girls that are being recruited. There's five or six of them that are in my main group chat that consistently come to workouts, consistently ask me questions, and things like that. But again, everything's optional. You don't have to come to Monday night workouts if you don't want to, but the girls that are being recruited are usually there and make an effort to kind of listen and stuff. I send out newsletters that I write myself with recipes and workouts that I just think are fun. It's something that I enjoy doing—connecting and loving on other Black women. So that's what I'm doing."

Loving on Black women requires a particular skill set. It requires the ability to practise self-love and a desire to engage in community care. Black women are not a monolith. We sit at an intersection of race and gender, with a distinct ability to recognize anything and everything that may marginalize people—class, ability, age, sexuality, immigration status, education, religion, and more—because many of us associate with a variety of these intersectional distinctions ourselves.

For Kim Davis, family, friends, and community keep her focused, humble, and happy. Ms. Davis knows she couldn't work in hockey without a diverse group of friends and family who support her trials and successes and help her stay grounded.

"It's so important, protecting your peace, and it has been important throughout my career at every moment of the different journeys I've been on. I have an amazing family support structure, you know?" She smiles. "Starting with my husband, who has been my greatest cheerleader and fanboy for the thirty-seven years that we've been married and the forty years that we've been together. That has meant a lot in terms of my feeling completely free to pursue my passions—as a mother, as a wife—and all of those roles have been important. That journey of raising my kids and having my kids while I was building my career could not have happened without a supportive partner. So that's been critical to my journey and my success. I have a daughter and a son, my daughter is married, and so I have a son-in-law and a grandson . . . and we are a close-knit family.

"I get a lot of energy from those relationships in this business. I learned a lot about millennials, particularly from my kids and the perspective that my kids have on . . . being Black in this world, and it allows me to never lose touch with reality. My son, who identifies as queer, also gives me a true insight on the perspective of being Black and queer, affluent and educated, and what that means in terms of how I should think about my engagement in the sport of hockey.

"I think about the future through the lens of my grandson, who is biracial. And, you know, I ask myself every day: *am I making hockey the kind of sport that I feel comfortable for him to be in?* That really is my litmus test of the work that I'm doing. Right? At the end of the day, I promise you, every day I say, *Have I done something today that's making hockey better for Liam?*"

Intersectional identities exist and people can be and usually are more than one thing. Authentic connections that recognize these dichotomies and that manifest in action, not mere words, are key to building equitable spaces in hockey. There is an opportunity for solidarity within not just Black communities, but among all marginalized folks who have traditionally been left out of hockey spaces. As an organization that advertises itself as a support system for Black women and all marginalized folks who support our mission, Black Girl Hockey Club works to bring that solidarity mindset to each and every meet-up, virtual event, and conversation we have. My ideal IRL Black Girl Hockey Club activity looks something like this: we start with a community event. Something that the locals can get into, because what it's really about is how the local hockey community treats these folks after we've left town. Let's invite some hockey players, the co-conspirators, and let's get some kiddos in the room, play some games, and learn about teamwork.

A BGHC pre-pandemic event with the Penguins' Tracey McCants Lewis and Delvina Morrow took place on Pittsburgh's first official Black Hockey History Day on January 31, 2020, and included playing ball hockey with the kids at Miller Elementary—the first public elementary school to offer an African-centred curriculum—located in Pittsburgh's Lower Hill District, a historically Black neighbourhood. That meet-up has been my long-time favourite (*Go Pens!!*), and I will forever endorse a model that includes hiring Black women to get the job done. Tracey and Delvina are committed to the city of Pittsburgh, and they are also committed to the Black communities there, and I'm proud to have them in my network of Black women in hockey.

What the Leafs did in Toronto with BGHC in April 2022 also goes into my mental PowerPoint presentation when I talk about what a really good community hockey event looks like. Toronto is incredibly diverse, and there are some really good people at Maple Leaf Sports and Entertainment (MLSE) who are committed to making authentic connections in local spaces. Mark Fraser, for example, is a young Black former pro committed to equity and inclusion in hockey. When Mark recognized a gap in how his home team addressed diversity and inclusion efforts, he reached out to then GM Kyle Dubas to pitch an idea and job description. The position of Director, Culture & Inclusion at the Toronto Maple Leafs was created, a role which Mark was born to fill. While Jen Reynolds no longer works with MLSE, at the time of this event she was the leader of the internal MLSE LGBTQ employee resource group and also the Senior Manager of Equity, Diversity and Inclusion during the 2021–22 season. Between the two of them, Jen and Mark made sure we secured the MLSE LaunchPad community facility for some floor hockey and an educational panel; they connected us to group sales at the Hockey Hall of Fame; they hosted a luncheon to honour Black women (it was literally called the "Women's Luncheon Celebrating Black Excellence in Hockey," which is an amazing name tbh) at which I got to meet Angela James and Bernice Carnegie (plus I had to do an impromptu speech in front of these icons after a glass of bubbly, so yeah, I almost died); and then they topped it off with tickets to a weekend Marlies game and seats for our BGHC squad of fifty at a Monday night Leafs game against Buffalo in the freaking Scotiabank Arena Gondola Box 6. This was definitely an invite-only weekend, because when BGHC goes into the community or has limited space, our invitations are intentional.

The reality is, hockey is predominantly white. If free activities or opportunities are put out there, even if they are centred on Black neighbourhoods or organizations, non-Black folks will always take advantage of them. We have to intentionally create and enforce a space for Black women and our co-conspirators. Anything less than 100 per cent clarity can create confusion and anger. While this type of intentionality may seem, at first glance, like gatekeeping, spaces dedicated to equity must take into account past (and current) discrimination in hockey and then compensate for it. Priority for the Toronto takeover started with our local scholarship girls and their families, our panellists and their families, then our volunteers, supporters, and co-conspirators. I got to meet so many people in person that I had only interacted with online, in the Slack volunteer chat, or in Zoom meetings, including some of our wonderful scholarship awardees and their parents. The entire whirlwind event was amazing, start to finish, for everyone involved, and I don't think I'm being hyperbolic.

Not only did she bring her gold medal to the community event at MLSE LaunchPad and let us basically walk around with it all day, Sarah Nurse also brought her dad to the game on Monday night, took pictures, and hung out with us all evening while wearing her custom Justin Bieber–designed Leafs jersey. Saroya Tinker and her partner, Danté Djan, showed up to the game in limited-edition BGHC jerseys created and donated by Gary Luisi—a Los Angeles–based BGHC volunteer—and then Danté proceeded to pump his girl's tires the entire time. Mark Strong, in-house MC/host of the Toronto Raptors and now Shireen Ahmed's husband, brought a dozen warm and wrapped roti and doubles from Leela's, his favourite in-arena vendor, so that the Muslims who were fasting for Ramadan had food at sunset for iftar, the evening meal. The event was beautiful, inclusive, and full of joyful moments that took my breath away.

Although I consider myself empathic, I am not a very sentimental person. I thrive on logic, order, and a good to-do list. But there is something about a Black Girl Hockey Club meet-up that makes my heart ache in the best way. It's hard to explain the emotion that ran through me watching the absolute joy on the face of one of our scholarship girls as she held Sarah Nurse's attention, gold medal dangling from her fingers as she spoke, keeping her audience of adult women hockey fans rapt with excitement as they recognized and validated her experiences playing a sport they all adored. It felt pretty epic, to say the least. This same girl's mother stopped to give me a hug at the LaunchPad event, and proceeded to tell me how important the scholarship award had been for her daughter's self-confidence and how much it meant to their family. She let me know that, at a turbulent time in their personal lives, the BGHC community, and especially Saroya Tinker and her mentees, had been a godsend for her daughter. Saroya had given her daughter rides, helped her with her hair, and checked in on them when no one else had bothered. With tears in her eyes, this mother thanked me not for the money, or the swag, or even the free game tickets. She thanked me for caring about them at a time when it seemed that no one in or out of hockey had given a damn about her kid—her words, not mine. I'm not ashamed to admit that I cried tears of joy that day, knowing that my dream of building a welcoming and safe community for Black women in hockey meant something to this family and this little girl.

I'm proud of the work that I've done with Black Girl Hockey Club, but creating community in hockey doesn't end with us. We provide an equitable space for marginalized fans and give folks an excuse to get together, talk hockey and watch games, find fellowship and make friends, and we hope that we can be an inspiration for organizations as large as the Toronto Maple Leafs and group chats as small as the Pronoun Gang. BGHC provides a blueprint for how to engage with local Black communities every time we organize an event online or in person. We try to show that utilizing a community-first, Black-women-led model in hockey can help build authentic connections that last a lifetime and grow the game exponentially. When we tout the concept of "hockey is for everyone," this is what it must mean. That all people, of any gender, sexuality, race, age, class, and ability are welcome not only to participate but also to thrive in the sport of ice hockey, at all levels, within a safe and equitable system.

Unfortunately, that system doesn't truly exist yet. In the meantime, we do our best work in the group chat, which actually represents our spaces, our communities, our circles.

We facilitate growth and change in those places. We do this together, because changing the world is always better with friends. And when things get difficult, as they tend to do, we search the internet for the perfect meme and then we send it to the GC. It won't make everything better, but it's a great place to start.

Road Fans

My work at BGHC requires that I authentically connect to multiple hockey clubs without bias, and so I can honestly say that I enjoy all the games and arenas that I've visited in this capacity. We have a good time, the teams are gracious and supportive, and I've been known to purchase team gear and wear it to games, even when it's not the Penguins! In my dresser, I've got beanies (toques?) from the Washington Capitals, Seattle Kraken, Vancouver Canucks, New York Rangers, Dallas Stars—and of course the Pittsburgh Penguins—which are all in regular rotation as soon as the weather permits. I've found that rainbow Pride team pins are a cheap and easy way to rally behind an organization while visiting their arena, and I have no problem putting one on and supporting a team that is partnering with BGHC to make space for Black girls in the sport of ice hockey.

But when I'm not travelling to see hockey games with BGHC, there is a particular barn I visit where I boo the home team, which is incredibly unprofessional and not very equitable of me.

I'm a hockey fan, I'm allowed to have mortal enemies, right?

When I go to this barn, I heckle the home team fans, because, obviously, their team sucks. I laugh when their forwards miss, and make fun of an eleven-game losing streak to the point where I have gotten cussed out by fans in the parking lot. I'm not sorry. I'm actually laughing out loud right now at the memory, especially because I have tickets to a game in this arena coming up in a few weeks!

One time, even though we lost the game, my companion hung their head out the passenger-side window and yelled, "Go Stars!" as we were leaving the parking lot, to which a home team fan replied, "Go home!"—which still makes me laugh to this day as the most clever chirp ever aimed in my direction.

There's something to be said about the resilience of visiting fans at a hockey game. And I'm a Black woman hockey fan! I've got to be fearless, right?

Everyone knows I'm a Penguins fan, and I have seen them play in a number of arenas. As a visiting Pens fan, *whew boy!* Folks really do hate us. And Sidney Crosby. Folks *despise* Sidney Crosby. It's ridiculous when you think about it, because he is actually the best modern hockey player since Gretzky, and I'd argue . . . Well, that's the point. I argue! As a travelling Pens fan who is a fat, Black, queer woman, I stand out, and I know this, so I lean into it and enjoy myself—because isn't that what being a fan is all about? I'm in my most natural state as a travelling Pens fan, because I'm full of spite *and* joy! Everyone also knows that when the Pens are on they are *on* (see: back-to-back Cup wins in 2016 and 2017), and even when they suck, they're still fun to watch, because they have Sidney Crosby and Evgeni Malkin.

Seeing the Pens play in their home arena is a transcendent experience, especially for a fan who only gets this team in my state once a season, but there's something to be said for the community of road fans. Rallying with strangers who have a shared love of the away team, and who are determined to enjoy a game in an enemy arena, can be kinda scary, but it's worth it because we all adore this silly game. Road fans follow our team into a space that actively does not want us there. We saunter into a home arena full of thousands of enemy fans, wearing the opposing team's colours with our heads held high and a fierceness in our stride. We gather on the wrong side of the arena for warm-ups, and cheer as loud as we can through the boos so that our team knows we're there for them. When the away team scores at those games, and road fans high-five each other or start a chant that upsets the home team fans so much they start to leave before the end of the third period? Well, there's nothing more satisfying than a hard-earned win on the road!

Just think about how much you hate seeing road fans in your arena when your team loses. I'm usually on the other side of that feeling, fam.

It's probably why I'm so good at my job as executive director of Black Girl Hockey Club. I walk into a boardroom or hockey space with mostly cisgender white men who have little to no desire to hear what I have to say about racism in the locker room or equitable hiring practices, and it feels kinda familiar. I hold my head up high, I know I've got a great team behind me, and I am confident that good will prevail. And when we win? When I get to walk into a room and share my story with folks who are empathetic to the experiences of marginalized fans and also passionate about the game? When we can discuss policy and move the needle in a way that is equitable and beneficial for Black folks? Well, those are the days when I am holding my head out of the proverbial passenger-side window, hollering with joy. Because, as hockey fans, we know that it isn't always about a single win; there is a journey to the Big W, right? Neither I nor my work with Black Girl Hockey Club is going to eradicate racism from hockey, let alone sports in general, not to mention the world or whatever. Not on my own. But when I find my fellow co-conspirators within the institutions—those brave, righteous folks who put themselves and their work on the line time and time again, in order to truly make hockey for everyone—well, those are my people. Warriors willing to challenge the status quo and to step into spaces where they might not be fully accepted, and where they are sometimes outright disdained, and still do the work.

Road fan toughness seeps into my bones, and it gives me strength.

SELF-CARE AS COMMUNITY CARE.
I'M TREATING *WE* RIGHT!

I am an angry Black woman. I read Audre Lorde, and I get angry. I watch the news, I get angry. I talk to my Black sisters and brothers in hockey about their experiences, and I get so damn angry I want to roll my eyes, scream, quit my job, and become a hobbit. I think J.R.R. Tolkien might have been a little racist, and then I get even more angry, because it seems the entire world since forever has been shit and there isn't anything I can personally do about it, so why even try? Then I get depressed. Not clinical depression, but a deep sadness that sits on my chest and makes me doomscroll social media endlessly while feeling more and more agitated and upset at the state of the world and all the things I'm unable to do to fix it. James Baldwin once said something along the lines of this: the more a Black person in America knows, the worse they feel. In my forty-fourth year on this planet, that has never felt more true. Ignorance certainly *seems* blissful.

I went to solo talk therapy for the first time just a few months before I turned forty. I had decided to pursue the concept of Black Girl Hockey Club in whatever shape it was going to take, and wanted to learn emotional balance and how to better handle my mental health. I had also started having panic attacks, and while meditation worked to an extent, I booked an appointment with one of the few Black woman therapists in my county who accepted my insurance and dedicated real time to learning how to treat myself, and my feelings, with a bit more care.

Audre Lorde tells us in her essay "Poetry is Not a Luxury" that "[F]eelings were not meant to survive. . . . We have felt them all already. . . . there are no new ideas. There are only new ways of making them felt . . ." Addressing our feelings takes away their mystery. Naming our feelings allows us to speak truth to the ideation behind our emotions. Lorde called that poetry.

I learned in therapy that I can only control myself, and that my feelings are valid whether they are rooted in history, facts, or simply my personal truth. All the meditation, massages, and retail therapy—by way of lower bowl hockey tickets—will not dull the immutable anger that hits me when hockey inevitably does something awful, like put into a position of power a man like John Vanbiesbrouck, who resigned as head coach of the Sault Ste. Marie Greyhounds and was banned by the Ontario Hockey League in 2003 after calling Trevor Daley, one of his own players, the fricken N-word. Despite this racist act, Vanbiesbrouck was hired by USA Hockey as Assistant Executive Director of Hockey Operations in 2018. The banner bearing Vanbiesbrouck's name and number was not removed from the Greyhounds' home rink until early 2024—more than twenty years after the incident. In a statement posted to social media by the Hockey Diversity Alliance, Daley said: "The one very dark and racist moment of my hockey career is something that I had to relive each time I returned to the Gardens and looked up to the rafters. The next time I enter the Gardens, look up, and [do] not have to relive one of the worst moments of my life eliminates a major source of anger and frustration for both me and my family."

With too many examples of racism, sexism, and misogynoir in hockey to list, suffice it to say discerning hockey fans have good reason to be angry at a sport that is still overwhelmingly white, and that historically marginalizes anyone who doesn't identify as a cisgender straight white male. And boy, does that anger make white people uncomfortable, defensive and, yes, angry.

My therapist would ask me, *How does your anger serve you, Renee?*

Lorde, in her 1981 essay "The Uses of Anger: Women Responding to Racism," calls on allies, specifically white women, and asks them to face the feelings of Black women and learn to live with these feelings without centring themselves. In an organization like BGHC, this concept is principal to the mission of care that surrounds all of our Black women members. Black Girl Hockey Club was born of community love, but it was also an act of self-care. I *needed* a community, so I built one. I didn't start BGHC out of anger, but rather a need to share the heavy burden of exclusion within hockey spaces and to gather with like-minded folks to help make hockey more equitable for all. We have our own space, and in this space we examine feelings instead of ignoring them; we talk about generational trauma instead of keeping it buried deep inside of us and passing it on to our daughters. We let our co-conspirators (allies who are not Black women) and our enemies (the racists, the haters, the ones who don't want us here) know that sometimes we are angry, that we are unconcerned with the guilt or fear that arises when we articulate our feelings, but we vow to work through these issues together. This community means to facilitate change in hockey, standing alongside those who can move past their own guilt and anger in order to get shit done.

That doesn't mean it's easy. In fact, parsing our emotional trauma and triggers is exhausting, long-term work that can feel like one step forward and ten steps back some days. Addressing bias, privilege, marginalization, and micro/macro-aggressions requires a deep dive into one's own psyche, and means asking questions of "nature vs. nurture" while examining environments such as family, school, church, friends, work, fandoms, and more. This means striving for a lifelong, global education.

For Black women, it is imperative to be cognizant of the stereotypes placed on us by society, and to recognize that the institutions we hold dear may not have our best interests at heart. Putting personal health above corporations and institutions is an act of self-care. Unapologetically taking up space is an act of self-love. Saying "no" is self-preservation.

Unfortunately, setting boundaries can often contribute to the stereotype of the "angry Black woman," which means that some of us are wary of applying them to our lives out of fear of retaliation. While *self-care* has recently become a societal buzzword, in reality it is a radical act when accomplished by Black women, simply because the world does not want us to rest, and society does not give Black women the opportunity to focus on ourselves and our own well-being. When we practise caring for ourselves, we are able to turn that self-love outward onto our communities, contributing to organized efforts while rethinking and rebuilding community spaces.

Hockey doesn't have to be awful. Racism can be eradicated. The policies can be more equitable. The game can be a safer, more diverse space for all marginalized folks. This is the message that I tell every single person who is willing to listen to me talk about hockey. Sports can be better, and they can be inclusive, but it will take every single person who is committed to equity to do everything they can every single day in every aspect of their life in order for change to actually happen. It sounds practically impossible, right? But the thing is, you consistently do what you can, where you are. That's it. You take care of yourself and your community, and the changes you are making in yourself will move outward into the spaces you occupy, until your self-love and community care touch everything and everyone you encounter, because you have intentionally made those efforts daily.

You're going to mess up, of course. We all do. Yes, even me! My therapist would ask me, *Renee, how can you use those mistakes to learn and grow?* When I push myself too hard and don't eat, sleep, or take care of my body and then I get sick; when I say yes to a project that I then do half-assed, with resentment; when I never tell that toxic friend or colleague that their words and actions have pushed me away, and instead harbour resentment and then just ghost them—ultimately, I'm hurting myself. There is no joy or peace for me if I don't stand up for my beliefs, for Black women, and for other marginalized communities. My self-care then becomes community care. It becomes something to teach and to share. I take this value of self and of connection to community with me into all my relationships, and hope that it is the one thing I convey with energy and purpose. I brought that determination into Black Girl Hockey Club, and I bring it to my writing now, in the hopes that you, dear reader, will walk away with a better understanding of what you can do to make the spaces you occupy equitable, safe, and fun for everyone.

Dr. Courtney Szto, Queen's University assistant professor and Black Girl Hockey Club volunteer, spends much of her time asking how she can serve others. So when the question of self-care and support systems comes up in one of our conversations, she is quick to take the spotlight off of herself. Dr. Szto's work examines Canada's national hockey system, particularly youth hockey, and is a call to action for Canadian hockey fans committed to equity in the sport. She comes to the sport as an academic, a hockey player, and a fan of the game.

"From a player standpoint, what I need from the hockey community is white folks to step up and to curtail certain locker room conversations that go on. I think the locker room is a wonderful space where you can have very open and honest conversations, or it can be a terrifying place. I just can't imagine what it's like for younger kids at this point," she muses.

"There was a situation about a year ago when COVID was starting to make its way over here. And a couple of white teammates were talking about it. And they're like, 'Queen's University, because the students are super racist, they had a COVID party.' This is when it was only in China, predominantly—like, people were dying in large numbers [of] COVID. *This* is what the kids do.

So [my teammates] were talking about this, and then one of [them] was like, 'It's kind of funny.'

"And I thought, *I'm gonna look down and tie my skates and I'm not going to engage in this conversation. I don't want to be part of it.* And finally, one of our other teammates, she stepped up, and she's like, 'Well, they're also picking on the kids at school, you know, like, it's not okay, it's creating a lot of racism, and it's not fair to those students.' And then the other women were like, 'Yeah, that's fair.' I bet you if I asked her, she wouldn't even remember that conversation. But I remember that she stepped up and said something. And so I think it's white folks just saying things like that."

Often it is women of colour who are community-building, creating space, and doing the work of educating and liberating minds, but that doesn't mean anti-racism work should be done exclusively by us. The support of allies, whether marginalized groups are in the room or not, is imperative to building community trust. Examining your own privilege, and understanding the fear and the anger that can come with addressing that privilege, leads to inner healing that can move outward.

As a non-Black woman and a volunteer for a Black-led organization, Dr. Szto recognizes that, in this space, her role requires listening, learning, and providing resources to further the mission and values of anti-racism in hockey and of Black Girl Hockey Club. When she joins BGHC committee calls, Dr. Szto admits, she feels closest to a "white person in a group." She defers to Black leadership with the knowledge that she is welcome, she is valued, but she doesn't have to be the loudest voice in the room. Contributing to anti-racism in hockey for Dr. Szto means participating in a network of agitators with whom she can pool resources in order to create a tangible culture shift in sport. Through community-building, the hockey space can become a place of joy, feeding a need for connection and becoming a source of nourishment and love, while also making hockey a better, safer sport for all.

"I definitely have a very good network of colleagues that I can vent to, and cause good trouble with. Getting to do fun projects and put together events with other *troublemakers*, as I like to call them." Dr. Szto laughs. "I think that that's really what kind of keeps you going. You just kind of collect people as you go along, and you collect more fun, cool people. And that's what keeps you going to do the work. What choice do we have? Really, it's either you walk away, and you don't watch or play hockey anymore, or you do something about it. So I think that it's kind of a false narrative that we make that choice, per se. I mean, obviously, we do make that choice. But it's a terrible choice, and not really a choice."

Hockey is full of cool people because it's a cool game, but there is so much work to be done in order to make it an equitable game for everyone. One of the biggest fallacies used against social activists can be boiled down to a single phrase: *If you don't like it, leave.*

Don't like America? Leave.

Don't like Canada? Leave.

Don't like hockey culture? Leave the sport to us, we don't want you anyway.

But that's not a choice at all, is it? Personally, I don't like institutions that uplift white supremacist values. I don't like misogynoir. I don't like racist, sexist, homophobic folks making the rules and writing the policies and telling me and other marginalized folks that we don't belong through their actions, their gatekeeping, and their perpetuation of the status quo. So how about instead of leaving, we take care of ourselves and our communities using the tools available to us? We can build up spaces in which we collectively support one another. We have the power to choose where we spend our money, what programs we support, and what institutions we engage with. We can invest in ourselves and in our communities, and create spaces in which we are able to thrive instead of scrambling to get a seat at their table. This is not cancel culture; this is accountability culture. This is the future.

During the summer of 2021, Naomi Osaka showed Black women everywhere how to practise self-care in real time, even as tennis fans and the media questioned her commitment, drive, and passion for her sport. While some saw Osaka's act of walking away from the French Open—and later the entire tennis season—due to mental health issues as weak, many Black women empathized with her decision to place herself and her personal health above the corporations representing tennis. The pressure of making this very personal decision in a very public sphere must have been overwhelming. What started as an act of self-care to protect her mental health quickly turned into a conversation about societal expectations, and if Osaka "deserved" the time off from tennis.

One of the only ways Black women are able to subvert discriminatory systems based in white supremacy is to practise radical self-care and to unequivocally support others who do the same. While Osaka faced immediate backlash in the tennis world, many athletes, journalists, and fans across other sports voiced their approval of Osaka's decision to put her holistic well-being ahead of her commitment to tennis.

"I think for Osaka, I was not surprised by the initial reactions that she got. I am a little bit surprised at the overwhelming athlete support that she has gotten—largely, it seems like, outside of the tennis world, though, which is funny, right? It's Black athletes in other spaces, and not necessarily tennis players, who have stepped up," Dr. Szto points out. "I think that it's been good to see and I think probably her withdrawing is perhaps the better option from an activist standpoint, but also from her own health standpoint. It really showed how serious she was because there were definitely people that I talked to in the tennis world who were like: *She's just milking this, she's got her endorsements. She's doing it at a tournament where she knows she's not going to do well, so it was not that big of a hit to her.* There was a lot of cynicism, and I was just really surprised, and I was like, *Is there anything that you have seen from Naomi before that looks like it would lead you to believe these things?*

"Federer pulled out because of his physical health a few days later. Obviously, that's very different, I think, because, you know, physical injury we accept, but the mental things are like, *Well, we can't see it, you should be pushing through it.* We all have it, even though we can't see the extent of it, and I think that that's really the problem. I'm hopeful that Naomi has really started a legitimate conversation around not only athlete mental health, but the ridiculousness of the press and the role of the beat reporter at sporting events. My hope is that a few years from now, I get to teach how Naomi Osaka was the starting point for a very new-looking sports environment, which would be really cool."

Not only did Osaka prioritize her own mental health and well-being, her act of radical self-care created a ripple effect in the sports world. Black women and other women of colour, athletes, journalists, and fans came out in support. Her decision to protect her own peace sparked conversations about mental health and the role that those who work in sports have in helping athletes maintain their minds as well as their bodies. A big part of these conversations centred on the pressure the media places on Black women athletes and the disparities between how they and white athletes are treated. Why is it that when Black women say "no," there are think pieces on whether or not we are allowed to do so, or whether it is the right place and time for that kind of resistance? Why are we expected to push through and power forward and disregard our own well-being in favour of that of our families? Or our companies? Our fandoms? Our countries? Is it because it isn't about the name on the back but the logo on the front? Or is it because of racist policies and tired tropes that require Black women to act as selfless mammies? We are supposed to put the oxygen mask on ourselves before we put one on anyone else. We cannot facilitate a shift in hockey culture until we create a shift in the way we treat ourselves and those around us. We cannot move forward as we always have. Change has to start somewhere, so let it start within.

According to Erica Ayala, independent sports journalist and owner of Black Rosie Media, the controversy around Naomi Osaka's withdrawal from the 2021 French Open sparked conversations on language, boundaries, and equitable policies around health. Erica is adamant that the clear boundaries Osaka set should have been respected by the media and protected by corporate policy. Without regulations that protect marginalized folks, self-care, community care, and the language around those concepts can be weaponized and used to subjugate and strip our rights.

"I'll start by saying that Naomi Osaka got me thinking more about my mental health and wellness. *Mental health* is not a term that I use for myself, personally," Erica clarifies. "I'm also starting to realize that that's likely because of conditioning, because of how language matters, and I do believe that language matters, but language is also weaponized. And language is often weaponized against Black women. And so, there's that. I'm working through that a little bit. Yeah."

Here Erica pauses. What I have learned about her is that she chooses her words very carefully. Erica is a top-notch Black Latina sports journalist from Harlem whose work has been featured in the *New York Times*, *Forbes*, *Sports Illustrated*, and the *Washington Post*. She comes from a family of educators, and holds a bachelor's degree in political science and a master's in public administration. Erica worked and excelled in the non-profit sector for a decade before she began a career writing about women's sports, where she continues to excel. When Erica Ayala puts words out into the universe, she does so with purpose.

"There is no part of me that read that screenshot [Naomi] posted, not as a journalist, as an adult, as a Black woman, as a human being, that found there needed to be any further explanation [beyond] what she offered. She, in her very Naomi way, you know, was like, *Hey, I know that this is different, I know that this will get me fined. But this is what I need for me.* And I read that she was accepting any repercussions that would follow and was open about that. And knowing that, she still made the choice that she did.

"So for me, again, now, as a Black woman, as a human being of the earth, and certainly as a journalist, it was extremely frustrating for me to hear across the gamut, whether you are a Black man or white woman, or anything in between and beyond, for people to request—excuse me, not *request*, to *demand*—that she make her statement sooner, that the way she and her team handled it was improper. Naomi's statement did not ring any of those bells for me.

"And you know, I talk about this with Black Girl Hockey Club when it comes to leadership development and volunteerism, because I'm taking human resources very seriously. I am energized by human resources. And it's because of issues like this."

Erica isn't lying. She loves policy! She sits on the committee for BGHC's "Get Uncomfortable" campaign, and specifically works on developing policy suggestions for signatories of the Get Uncomfortable Pledge and the official GUC playbook. Erica has also moderated a number of BGHC panels, and brings her expertise into every aspect of her anti-racism advocacy. For Erica, equitable policy based on the tenets of intersectionality is the key to creating true change in hockey.

"When Naomi Osaka said, *I'm dealing with mental health*, she gave more than she needed to; more than what was required. If you're sick—you could have strep throat, you could have diarrhea, or you could be going to freeze your eggs—all you say is, 'I'm taking a sick day.' Period. Now, your boss can ask . . . because they want to guilt people into not taking time [off], but don't believe the hype! Fight the funk! We do not have to give that information.

"And it's just so troubling to me that we're coming off of a pandemic where nobody wanted to be like, *Oh, so-and-so has a positive* COVID *test*, because apparently we understood the separation of health and privacy when it came to COVID. But when it comes to mental health, now, it's like, *Well, are you schizophrenic? How? When were you diagnosed bipolar? Are you on medication? Are you just saying this? Or do you have a diagnosis?* All these questions; it's exhausting.

"The grace with which Naomi has moved through this entire situation is inspiring, and has me again identifying for myself: *What are my personal and professional barriers? What are the things that I need to do for the sake of my mental wellness? My wellness overall? Where [do] I need to set boundaries?* And for me, that has been the biggest takeaway personally, and I hope outside of even just me as an individual. That's something that I am going to take as a journalist."

Self-care ultimately requires confronting and managing our own mental and physical health, and, as counterintuitive as it may sound, practising true self-care requires that we think beyond our own personal experiences and recognize our privileges in comparison to those around us. It requires addressing community conditions and institutional policies, examining the way society treats Black women and other marginalized groups, and understanding how this discrimination affects our mental health. For Erica, that means examining her own expectations as a journalist, as well as using her skills to support organizations that value the well-being of her community. When we look inward to understand ourselves and our own motivations, we are then able to use our power and privilege to help create spaces, policies, and opportunities that allow others that same thoughtfulness.

The knowledge that we cannot go through our existence on this planet as solitary beings is essential to the mental health of folks who engage in advocacy. Historically, Black women in hockey did not have a dedicated community space before BGHC, which speaks to the necessity of community and the importance of this fun, engaging, anti-racist organization. But that's not the only significance of community when it comes to the work we do. If the goal is to create space for those who come after, it will take all of us—shifting, moving, and changing the way that we deal with the world—to make that space. None of us are perfect, and none of us can do it alone.

Blake Bolden, the first-ever Black woman professional hockey player, who played in both the NWHL and the CWHL, is pretty firm on how she practises self-care. For Blake, saying "no" and unplugging are essential parts of protecting her peace, as is maintaining a strong sense of community.

"Honestly, having a support system is one of the best sounding boards too, because you're going through life and things happen so fast, and you can make a decision and it can be wrong, and that's totally fine. You can make a wrong decision and go through some stuff. But it really helps to not step on those landmines because you've got someone to say, *Okay, well, why are you doing this? If you do this, then this will happen, or, if you don't do this, this will happen.* I think, for the people that don't have that, it makes life so much harder; if you don't have a mom that you can rely on, or a dad that inspired you to do something that you never thought you could do, or a partner that, you know, motivates you and keeps you honest, or someone that you can call and ask for business advice—that makes life so much harder. You can't do life by yourself. You can't. We're social beings. It's literally a physical impossibility to do life by yourself."

The statement hits me hard when I think about the fact that Blake spent four years playing hockey at Northwood School in Lake Placid as the only Black person on campus. The healing that she has found comes from a support system that understands that individual wellness begins with community mindfulness. It is within this community that Blake has found her voice, as well as the encouragement and the strength to make a difference in hockey.

We cannot forget that healing can be uncomfortable and some folks may unintentionally (and intentionally) create roadblocks to personal and community success, because it is easier for things to stay the same than for things to change, even when those changes are for the better. Melissa Williams is a Cuban-Peruvian American from Southern California who works as a licensed marriage and family therapist at La Sierra University. Melissa and I went to college together, and we have been friends for almost twenty years. I consulted with Melissa often when it came to writing this book. As a practising therapist on a college campus, she consistently serves a variety of cultural groups. Together, we are co-conspirators on campus, working together so that LGBTQ, Black, brown, and all marginalized students have mentors and safe spaces at our parochial PWI. We both agree that you must do what you can do in your own space.

"As you engage in self-care—in boundary-making, in learning about self and acknowledging needs, and engaging in activities and things that fuel you and feed your soul, all of those self-care activities—as you do that, naturally, the people around you begin to notice that something is different. Usually, it's positive, sometimes it's pushback, particularly when all of a sudden, I'm setting up new boundaries, and it feels like I'm pushing you away. Right?" Melissa is prompting me through the screen as we talk. I nod, make eye contact, and she keeps going. She's probably such a good therapist!

"I don't practise in a hole by myself; I practise in real life. And so as I get healthier, those around me notice and are aware that I am healthier. Part of it is that I engage in my roles with more intentionality, with more energy. You can tell when I'm over it and I don't want to be here and I'm here out of obligation, compared to when I am here, ready to give you the attention and the energy that you deserve.

"We tend to push back as a community when things are different, but we cannot grow, we cannot move, we cannot change without a certain amount of discomfort. Be gracious with yourself and your journey and your movements and your behaviours and your expectations and how you go through life. Show the grace to yourself that you give those that you care for the most and that you value the most, because we're typically very harsh on ourselves. In giving ourselves that grace, we actually give ourselves an opportunity to flourish.

"The better care I take of myself, the better I can engage in those relationships and those things that are important to me. So the better care I take of myself, the better mother I am; the better care I take of myself, the better partner I am; the better care I take of myself, the better friend I am; et cetera, et cetera, et cetera. And so, if I think you are worth my time and are important and deserve the best of me that I can give, then I need to take care of *me*."

Self-care leads to community care, and community care ultimately leads to community healing. Creating and maintaining boundaries, holding myself and others accountable, and learning how to identify and manage my emotions have led me to a place where I can use my privilege and my resources to uplift others in the community as a part of my own growth and holistic well-being. On a micro-level, self-care as community care can look like organizing the carpool to a hockey game, dropping off dinner for a neighbour who has COVID, or asking people their pronouns and how to correctly pronounce their name. On a macro-level, it can include donating money or time to a social services organization, voting in local and national elections, and joining or starting a support group. At work, this type of community care can look like examining exclusionary hiring practices like unpaid internships, or evaluating the lack of representation in the boardroom.

I model grace, respect, and care by offering it to myself first, and then bringing that same energy to the folks in my community. I listen to my body and my spirit, I rest and encourage resting. I follow the work of the Nap Ministry, a movement of rest resistance centred in Black liberation started by Tricia Hersey. I deleted the Twitter app from my phone. I also spent last summer travelling, sleeping, and eating amazing food while celebrating my friends, my family, and myself. I accomplished one of my life goals and wrote this damn book.

As I write this chapter, I am on the last few days of a four-week vacation from all things BGHC and work-related; this is a break for all BGHC staff and volunteers, giving us the chance to unplug and reflect on our commitment to anti-racism in hockey. Then, with a renewed commitment and a nice summer tan, I and the other BGHC staff will return to the difficult work of anti-racism in hockey, refreshed and ready to conquer the never-ending shitshow that is hockey culture—and we will do it as a community.

WE'RE BLACK ALL YEAR LONG,
NOT JUST IN FEBRUARY

When folks ask me how I came to hockey, the short answer is "I'm a fan of being a fan." To me and anyone who knows me, this means I have overt obsessions that take over my life for a period of time. As an adult, I thoroughly enjoy spending my money and energy on things that bring me joy. When I was in college, this meant starting a writers' club on campus, or joining the English honour society and travelling across the country to read a twenty-page paper on feminism and death in Mary Shelley's *The Last Man* at a conference at the Westin in downtown Pittsburgh. After college, this love of fandom manifested in writing for various pop culture blogs so that I could travel to comic cons as press to interview some of my favourite actors, artists, and celebrities. My number-one fandom is the *Supernatural* fandom, of course (#SPNFamily, love 'em or hate 'em, family don't end with blood), and I've done unmentionable things in the name of fictional characters Dean and Cas over the last decade—and will continue to do so for the foreseeable future. My favourite genre of fan studies, though, is transformative works. From literature like Sir Arthur

Conan Doyle's Sherlock Holmes stories to the discourse around sports, I'm fascinated by the way that talented fans use quality content to create incredibly powerful artwork, fiction, film, and fan spaces.

I've always been a lit and film geek; so much so that popular culture ingrained in me that nerds and jocks just don't mix. It wasn't until I was innocently strolling through early 2010s Tumblr that hockey even became a tangible thing to me, and it was, funnily enough, a hockey comic that did it. All of a sudden, sports and nerdom mixed and I got curious. I wanted to be in on the good times, but I had no clue as to what was going on in the story because I had no clue about hockey.

Well, I'm nothing if not dedicated to being a fan, so I reached out to my friend Liz Koetting (formerly "San Diego Liz"), a fellow pop culture fangirl/writer from Wisconsin, with whom I had spent many hours over the years in the San Diego Comic-Con Hall H lines to see Jensen Ackles, Misha Collins, and the tall one (just kidding, I adore JarPad). Liz is a fandom friend and a co-conspirator from the good old days—when *Supernatural* had new episodes and the thought of COVID among con-goers hadn't ever occurred to us. I can and have left long video messages on Instagram for Liz at all hours of the day and night in a frantic state over (fictional character) Dean Winchester, and she doesn't question me, she just goes with it. This is the power of fandom!

Liz is also a sports fan, which at first seemed incongruent with what I understood to be fundamental pop culture truths. I've since come to understand that sports fandom and general nerd fandom are just two sides of the same geeky coin. There are fan cons, meet-ups, artwork, statistics, speculation, merchandise, podcasts, toys, academic papers, comics, fan vids—come on! It's so obvious, even if nerds and jocks never want to admit it. So when I stumbled into the hockey fandom, I did so as a media-savvy Blerd who had spent the last decade online in fan spaces participating in geek culture in a variety of ways. What I found was what I often find in fandom spaces, at least at first—a white-cis-male-dominated space with very little representation of queer, Black, or Indigenous people. But then, when I started in the *Supernatural* fandom, I didn't think there were any Black girls there either, it just took a little time to find them! I was determined to do so in hockey, as well.

Black Girl Hockey Club grew out of that desire, but as I moved forward with the concept—a group of Black girls hanging out and going to hockey games together—I realized that we, as individual fans working in a variety of fields, actually had so much more to offer hockey culture. I have met so many talented, intelligent, intuitive, empathic, savvy, professional Black women who rally for ice hockey, for The Culture, and for each other. With BGHC, the goal is to work together and pool our resources and skills in order to cultivate an inclusive and equitable community space—by Black women for Black women—in the sport we all love.

As I get older, I want to share the spaces that I love with the generations after me, and encourage young people to continue cultivating my favourite fandoms. I refuse to gatekeep anyone because of my own jealousy, pride, or sense of entitlement because I was "here first." We should want to make our fandoms as inclusive as possible, so that they will continue to thrive even as we move on from these spaces. For Black girls in hockey, that meant creating something from scratch, which is what we have done as a collective. From Bernice Carnegie to Saroya Tinker, Black women have carved out a space for themselves in hockey.

As I write this, multimedia sports platforms are aflutter with Black Girl Magic. Erica Ayala calls the play-by-play on the regular for women's hockey, basketball, and soccer; Brianna Rhone, who started out as the BGHC social media maven, recently got a job working with the USA Hockey socials; Jo Dabney, former BGHC in-house graphic designer, has created digital art for teams across various hockey leagues; Blake Bolden is all over ESPN; and even I got to do some colour commentary during the 2021 Winter Olympics for the women's hockey tournament on CBC Sports. There are Black girls who get together outside of BGHC formal events and go see hockey games together; they've got their own podcasts and Substacks and even non-profits! But while this waterfall of Black talent may have come into the spotlight of the current hockey fandom scene after BGHC, in reality, BGHC is a collective that uses our platform to document and spread awareness of Black hockey excellence to a larger mainstream audience, via Twitter, Instagram, our website, and our newsletter, and we do so with intentionality and action. As Mads Mikkelsen's Hannibal (fictional character) would say, *This is my design.*

In order for hockey to be accessible to the masses and to grow, hockey needs to move into the twenty-first century. That means utilizing technology to create inclusive spaces for marginalized people and addressing the lack of diversity within all aspects of the game—whether on the business side or the playing side. It means tapping into what is already a diverse part of the fanbase and engaging with us on our level and on our terms, in order to truly create a sport that is for everyone. It means HIRING AND PAYING BLACK PEOPLE to use our talent and skill to make hockey better for everyone.

Truth be told, this is easier said than done. One of the first things a long-time Black hockey fan said to me was that this sport moves at a glacial pace. New rules, new norms, and new partnerships evolve incredibly slowly. And yet, just months after they hired Tracey McCants Lewis and Delvina Morrow, my beloved Pittsburgh Penguins became the first NHL team to hold a publicized theme night celebrating Black hockey history in their community, inviting Black Girl Hockey Club to take part and help shape the community engagement. I firmly believe that the concept succeeded because Black women get shit done! More than 500 people purchased tickets through the link on the Penguins website, and Black locals began to develop a relationship with the team that hadn't existed before this very intentional act. Starting with our morning in the community playing ball hockey with a local elementary school, the activities the team put on made new fans and fostered long-term, authentic connections with the local population. The event and BGHC became an access point into hockey for Black yinzers, while allowing Black women to showcase our talent and business savviness in hockey spaces that had previously been closed to us.

Without Delvina and Tracey, the Pittsburgh Penguins might not have ever considered engaging with BGHC and Black fans, simply because without Black folks in the room, who is there to prioritize our communities? Our leaders? Our talent?

In 2019, the same year BGHC hit the scene as a non-profit, the American Legacy Black Hockey History mobile museum, curated by the NHL's Kim Davis, hockey documentarian Kwame Mason, and American Legacy Network's Rodney J. Reynolds, took its first tour across North America, with one of the first stops being our event in Pittsburgh. Prior to 2019, the concept of a league-wide celebration of Black hockey history was unheard of, even though the National Hockey League had celebrated its 102nd birthday and Black History Month its forty-third anniversary that very same year. In fact, many NHL teams sit in the middle of very diverse cities, but you wouldn't know it from entering their hockey arenas. From the Blue Lives Matter theme nights to hockey's obsession with the very racist and misogynistic media company Barstool Sports, the in-arena and online experience for Black fans, particularly Black women, doesn't seem to have ever truly been considered by the white men who populate the C-suites of hockey ops. These higher-ups haven't yet seemed to wrap their minds around the fact that Black women love hockey, we have money to spend, and we have claimed hockey as our own, for better or for worse.

Luckily, digital technology has made it so that hockey fandom has the opportunity to evolve using readily available tools, apps, and websites. The ability to communicate without borders allows marginalized communities—LGBTQ, Black, Muslim, and women-led organizations—to develop authentic ways to engage in growing the sport in those spaces and connect with what the hockey folks in charge like to call "non-traditional audiences" (a.k.a. not a white, straight, cis, able-bodied male). We've got our own podcasts, blogs, fan merch, and watch parties, while, frankly, the professional leagues often refuse to develop along with the tech or the fandoms and struggle to stay relevant. While the white girls behind many of our favourite hockey teams' social media accounts are cool and fun, they're not for or from The Culture. After the discouraging decision by the NHL in 2023 to ban players from wearing themed jerseys on the ice and the shift from the curated Black Hockey History mobile museum to the "United by Hockey" exhibit, it's hard to tell where Black women belong in hockey. This is why organizations like Black Girl Hockey Club are so vital to the continued movement of inclusion initiatives at all levels of hockey. It's up to us to plant the seeds so that these connections continue to grow.

Dr. Tunisha Singleton, BGHC board president and media specialist, studies the connections between fandom and media, and came to BGHC as a multi-sport fan excited about the ways that our org uses digital technology to engage with marginalized hockey fans. In her Ph.D. dissertation, titled "Digital Fandemonium," Dr. T, as I like to call her, discusses how the sports experience has to become multi-dimensional and how social media and digital communication strengthen a fan's commitment to a sport.

I met Dr. T in the fall of 2019. The Los Angeles Kings had invited me and another board member to a game right before the end of the previous season, in anticipation of building a robust partnership which still thrives today. A few months later, I invited locals to join BGHC and the Kings for our first official meet-up as a non-profit in Los Angeles, and Tunisha, along with about twenty others, answered the call. Now, Dr. T actually grew up only a few streets away from where I now live in Southern California, and her parents still live in my neighbourhood. Even now, I don't know that many Black hockey fans in the area, so meeting Tunisha brought me a singular joy that I hadn't felt before. *She's smart, she's funny, she loves Black culture, and hockey!? I want to know this woman!* And what stands out about Tunisha to me, and why I worked really hard to get her on the BGHC board of directors in 2020, is her love of fandom and her academic engagement with sports. I'm a sucker for a Blerd, and Dr. T is a young, hip, highly intelligent pop culture expert—particularly when it comes to sports.

When Tunisha rolled into that 2019 LAK X BGHC meet-up by herself, wearing her new BGHC original logo T-shirt, and befriended not only me but others in our group as well, I knew she was something special. That afternoon, she posted a selfie of her driving in her T-shirt to the game, tagged it #BGHC, and posted it on Twitter, a platform that BGHC uses as a primary communication tool to connect with other Black girl hockey fans. Of course, I retweeted it, and eventually posted that picture on the BGHC Instagram to encourage wider audience engagement.

Dr. Singleton's built-in audience—a mix of academics, jocks, and nerds interested in all types of sports—created a direct connection to a wider sports space that is often oversaturated by cis white fans. At a time when BGHC was establishing itself as a community space for all who support our mission, Tunisha's vocal online advocacy and digital support of BGHC helped push us to a new level of success on social media. When she expressed interest in volunteering with BGHC, I invited her to interview for a board position, and she stepped right into it. As the 2020 pandemic forced sports leagues to rethink fan engagement, technology, and social justice issues, Dr. T helped raise BGHC to new heights in order to address these issues head on.

With the onset of COVID in early 2020 and the murder of George Floyd, like many organizations BGHC pivoted to a more obviously socially conscious space. We used the summer break from hockey that year to fortify an org-wide desire to move forward in our programming using an anti-racist lens. Along with the rest of the world, we also had to figure out the best way to keep up with our audiences by utilizing technology as our main source of engagement. We began to use our social media accounts and our newsletter to encourage people in hockey spaces to examine how they were engaging with Black folks, while also offering paid digital services on topics pertaining to Black players and fans to hockey orgs that asked for our help. With Tunisha at the head of the board and many volunteer committees set up, we crafted a public-facing digital services product we could offer to hockey organizations, a product that centres Black women in hockey spaces. We also worked to build a leadership and development program that includes mentorship opportunities and master classes around hockey opportunities for young Black professionals of all genders.

When we finally get the chance to sit down together to talk about this book, I am curious about what Tunisha has learned by connecting her academic work around fan engagement with a community-building organization like BGHC. Turns out there is something to be said for having the ability to synthesize information for the masses in a digestible way. In the early days of our online presence, Dr. Singleton recognized a gap in how hockey culture engaged with BGHC and decided to use her academic skills to help fill that gap. Whether it is tapping into niche resources and sharing the bullet points or using learned knowledge to help create a road map to social equity in sports, Tunisha is well aware of the power of properly curated, shared information.

"The answers are out there," she says. "This is an example of companies sincerely wanting to find information, especially given the subject. And they want, they *need* help. This is how it should look; it should just be super digestible. No one will read my dissertation. *I* didn't read my dissertation. It's just fucking sitting over there and gathering dust. It's 150 pages of something no one will read. But people have read the reports that I took from my dissertation, because that's shareable, you can read that on the can. It's pretty, it's got pictures, and it's got bullet points.

"I keep reminding myself that I don't have to come up with the answers," Dr. Singleton reiterates. "Because no one knows the answers. We can only make more informed decisions. Look at patterns of like: *What's been happening before? What's fucked up? How can we fix it?* I think that's what innovation is. Innovation is not test tubes with blue liquid and beakers and smoke and shit. It's not chemistry; it's problem solving. Innovation is just finding a need and filling it. I don't have to find the answers. I just have to know where to look and who to ask."

Respectfully, Dr. T makes digitizing equity in hockey spaces sound much easier than it is. But then again, she is a whole *doctor*, and this general subject was part of her Ph.D. thesis. How Black women educate ourselves and how we choose to disseminate information is intentional and unique; understandably so, seeing as we are the most educated demographic in the United States. You see, Black women and marginalized folks all over the globe, in at least the fields of study that I have been a part of—academia, sport, and media—have made understanding and distributing information about equity a priority; because without parity, Black folks, LGBTQ folks, and disabled folks, among many others, lose out. We were not born knowing how to parse information, how to research our sources, how to shop mindfully, how to start non-profits or make hockey a safe space for Black women or any other marginalized group. We put in the work to educate ourselves and then move to action, because not only do we benefit, but others who share our intersectionalities— and even those who do not—will also reap the rewards of a safer, more equitable workplace, school, or home. We are Black all year long, for our entire lives, until we die! We wear our intersections on our skin and in our hair. We cannot only care about social justice issues during a single month of the year and then move on. We engage with purpose and an emotional intelligence that allows us to empathize with others, which is why we say *when Black women are free, all will be free.*

Not only is this type of intentionality important and necessary, with rewards for generations to come, but often, if marginalized folks do not rise up and voice our concerns and then offer our assistance on how to "fix" the "problem" of racism (or ableism, or homophobia, et cetera, et cetera), the status quo and the issues there remain the same. Hockey is filled with fans who love the sport and want to feel that the game has a place for them. That's why I'm doing the work—to create a sense of belonging that doesn't exist for Black women in the form that hockey currently takes. That's why Nathaniel Mata started RGV Roller in the Rio Grande Valley; he wanted access to hockey not only for himself, a Black Muslim in Texas, but for his community, because he loves the game. It is the same reason that Jazmine Miley launched the Hockey Players of Color Movement, so that she can play in tournaments and mentor BIPOC kids who love the sport as much as she does. It's why I started BGHC, and why Dr. Singleton took on the role of board president. Because these types of spaces didn't exist for us coming up in our favourite fandoms, but they are necessary for the growth of these things that we love.

For Mohamed Fofana, Group Sales Account Manager for the San Jose Sharks, the need for a diversity, inclusion, and belonging initiative at his workplace became imperative after the murder of George Floyd. He offered his expertise as a Black man to the hockey community because no one had yet picked up that mantle. Blake Bolden did the same with the Los Angeles Kings; Tracey and Delvina did it with the Penguins. But the work isn't easy. It might seem from the outside that we are just sharing or teaching from our experiences, but this requires emotional intelligence, vulnerability, and the patience to endure the precise kind of marginalization and tokenization we are building these spaces to avoid. Which is why organizations built *by* marginalized folks *for* marginalized folks are so valuable. BGHC is meant to centre Black women. That means making sure that everything from the events to the anti-racism work we do in hockey spaces honours that mission, that we don't add extra or unpaid labour to any Black person's load (particularly Black women), and that we engage mindfully and connect with other organizations and people who recognize that "ally is a verb," as my friend Shireen Ahmed always says, and not a descriptor you can slap on your Twitter bio to make you look more "woke." If Dr. T is giving you her best, if she is cultivating information for your company and putting it in a shiny, easy-to-read PowerPoint, you better pay that woman in cold hard cash, not "exposure"—cause exposure don't pay the bills!

With BGHC, Black women have connected to create our own community space using our varied skills. Dr. Singleton is only one example of the different types of expertise within our volunteer and supporter pool. Her success in this space validates my *very* controversial opinion that one does not have to be born with a hockey stick in hand in order to work and contribute positively to hockey spaces. Often in hockey, a person having previously played the game is a measurement of success, on both the business and media sides of the sport. Look at how many former players become coaches, GMs, owners, media pundits, or television personalities, not necessarily because they have the skills or training but because they played the game and have a "high hockey IQ" and a connection to a club. This in itself is a type of gatekeeping, because for its first one hundred years, professional hockey has systematically pushed out BIPOC and lower-income communities.

For many Black folks who have never played, hockey as a sport seems an insurmountable challenge—it's expensive, it's not easy to gain physical access to, and it seems kinda racist. Plus the league is very white, the fans are very white, and the staff are very, very white. So what's the point? Without an active, authentic attempt to engage with Black communities, hockey is left to white people, mostly players or former players. This leaves little to no room for innovation or diversity of thought, let alone actual melanin. I will never have hockey credentials from my playing years (full disclosure: I can't even skate and I don't want to learn), but that doesn't mean I don't have the skills to make hockey more accessible and ultimately more profitable, if that's the angle the bigwigs want to take. What I do have, and what many Black women bring to our work *and* our fandoms, are a savvy intelligence and a community-oriented work ethic that allows me to participate in creative problem-solving and benefit multiple stakeholders. What sport needs the creative and innovative problem-solving skills of Black women more than ice hockey?

Before I deleted the Twitter app from my phone to write this damn book, I would sometimes find myself scrolling through the comments under a BGHC post on that beloved hellsite. A persistent troll "question" would go something like this: *What if there was a white boy hockey club? That would be RACIST! YOURE THE REAL RACIST!!!!!!!*

I am, of course, paraphrasing, dear reader, but the sentiment is there. Sometimes I would catch the responses left by my allies, feisty friends I can picture in my mind's eye right now. I learned long ago not to answer the trolls myself, mostly because I catch feelings and you can catch these hands, but also because it isn't my job to convince people that I deserve nice things. But this kind of question has remained consistent over the years, appearing on various platforms where I have shared my hockey work, and it strikes me as hilarious every time I see it. Really, fellas? Have you taken a look at the sport lately? The whole thing is a white boy hockey club! We're just trying to stake a claim to a public sport that we happen to enjoy. What's all the hoopla about?

But in reality, the reason BGHC exists is because I need it to, and that should be reason enough. And the reason we are called "Black Girl Hockey Club" is because I didn't want anyone to forget that the mission and purpose of this tiny organization is to centre Black femmes in a very white, cisgender, straight, able-bodied, male space. Because we have never been acknowledged in this space before, and because when we are given the opportunity to flourish, we are able to do some truly amazing things.

For BGHC scholarship award winner Dayton O'Donoghue, finding other Black women in the sport that she loves has been a game changer. The support and care that the community has shown Dayton allows her to thrive as she achieves her goals both in hockey and outside of it. When I sit down one day with Dayton to talk about her experiences in hockey before and after finding BGHC, she gets candid.

"To be honest, as a Black female in the sport of hockey, you're kind of just programmed to think, *Okay, I'm alone in this. I've got myself to depend on in this game, I've got myself to depend on in this room, and that's it.* Even at the training things that I go to, it's pretty much all heavily the same crowd—all boys—and you kind of have to program yourself to think, *Okay, no one's going to be here picking me up. I've got to be everything that I need for myself.* But the Black Girl Hockey Club and Saroya's mentorship program really reminded me like, No, *there's a whole community that is rooting for you, that is standing behind you.* And just having that assurance that, you know, if I fall and it seems really, really hard to get up on my own, I'll have someone that's going to be there to help me. BGHC is going to support me when I don't know how to keep going. The resources that they have, just having that community to talk to, it goes a really, really long way.

"And it's truly a community I didn't know that I needed until I had it. It's not something that I truly thought about until I was immersed in that community and realized like, *How did I ever go on without having the support system with me?* I think having a strong mentor that looks like you and has travelled a path that you want to take, exactly like Saroya, is absolutely pivotal to staying on your path and staying focused and just pursuing your calling even when there are so many doors and so many obstacles in front of you."

The scholarship recognition and mentorship with Saroya Tinker has proved invaluable to Dayton, and just goes to show that a little community love goes a long way. Dayton applied for a BGHC scholarship in the fall of 2020, and was not awarded any cash then but was encouraged to apply again in the winter 2021 cycle. She did just that, and with an even stronger application, Dayton received our largest award, a $5,000 scholarship. Then, a year later, she received another $1,000 gift from BGHC. Between the two scholarships, Dayton connected with the Saroya Strong Mentorship Program, and began to grow her local community of supporters within hockey. In 2022, Dayton launched a partnership with Bauer Hockey and became one of the faces of their campaign "The Barn," which focuses on diversifying the game of hockey across Canada. With this opportunity, Dayton secured a

$100,000 Bauer Hockey equipment donation for Black Girl Hockey Club. This means we can give away a ton of new, high-quality hockey equipment to Black girls all over the world.

After a video of Dayton stickhandling went viral on social media in January 2022, she was invited to be a celebrity judge at the NHL All-Star Game. That summer, Saroya Tinker helped Dayton enrol in an elite summer skate program with college scouts in attendance, and in the winter, Dayton announced her intention to play NCAA hockey at Dartmouth College, an Ivy League school in New Hampshire. She started at Dartmouth in fall 2023, and continues to excel while remaining an active part of the BGHC community and building up those who are coming up after her. All of this from our little non-profit organization recognizing Dayton's skill set and creating a platform to highlight her hard work. There are so many possibilities for Black Girl Magic to shine through in hockey, and I'm determined to make sure that players like Dayton get the chance to play hockey, or to be in and around the sport, as long as they want to.

While the recognition of the skills and hard work of Black women from the NHL and other professional leagues is great, it is also just the beginning of how hockey culture can and should uplift Black women in this space. The work of Black women has been pivotal in the growth of the game in marginalized communities, and under the leadership of people like Kim Davis, Dr. Tunisha Singleton, Delvina Morrow, and others, hockey culture is shifting to be more inclusive and accessible to all. But honestly, community care is the gift we should give ourselves in these spaces where consideration for those who are

Othered hasn't previously existed! During times when inter-sectional voices calling for multifaceted restorative justice continue to be systematically oppressed by unjust laws and practices all over the globe, it is more important than ever that those working toward equity for marginalized groups stand together. In our unity comes strength as well as healing. Young women like Dayton will benefit from the emotional support of community and the tangible support of the programs our space offers. They will begin to see themselves on the ice and in the stands and behind the benches and in the C-suites, and they will gain confidence from this representation. They will begin to work in these spaces, and continue to shift pol-icy, diversify the boardroom, and mentor other young Black women with similar goals and dreams; and they will not only benefit from the infrastructure we are building now, but will make it even better in the future than you or I can imagine.

And what about me? I often get asked what I get out of this work, since I'm not a lifelong hockey fan and I don't play! What I get is the opportunity for fellowship, building relation-ships, and sharing my love of hockey with folks with similar experiences and backgrounds. I've always said that building BGHC was a selfish endeavour, and I mean that in the simplest way. I wanted friends, a fandom, to share this very cool sport with. I saw a need and I'm trying to fill it, mostly because pushing my Blackness aside to engage in hockey leaves me feeling isolated and lonely.

And that's the unspoken crux. In order to find success in hockey spaces, Black fans, players, and workers end up mini-mizing our Blackness in order to fit in and make those around us more comfortable, which makes it really difficult to build community. But it's not just in hockey, though, right? This happens in PWIS (predominately white institutions) from academia to journalism to tech to hockey. BGHC and the public work that I do across hockey is the product of me feeling incredibly tired of minimizing myself to fit in just so I can take part in the activities I love. I want my Blackness, my womanhood, and the social issues that affect me and the people I care about to be centred in the spaces that I occupy. Even though I am *just* a hockey fan, I want to be myself and still matter. And that's why there isn't a "white boy hockey club." There doesn't need to be. White supremacy has made it so that a white man will get the benefit of the doubt that a Black woman will not receive. He can love a thing and no one will question his commitment, no one will ask for his fan cred, no one will make him prove his worth, time and time again, just to be part of the *thing*. But if a fan is a Black woman, racism and misogynoir get added into the mix, and if she identifies as part of the LGBTQ community, homophobia or transphobia can be activated too. In too many spaces, whiteness and cisgender able-bodied maleness is considered the median or neutral identity. For too long, this has been what intersectional identities are measured against, and everything else tips the scales against what is "normal."

For me, being a fat, queer, biracial woman means that my credentials get questioned in almost any space I enter. From peers questioning my commitment to my master's program because I worked full-time and went to classes part-time (because capitalism), to the dude at the mall quizzing me on my favourite Doctor when I compliment him on his *Doctor Who* shirt, to the man at the hockey game who speaks over me to get to my male companion because the stranger thinks that the dude I'm sitting with has to be the hockey fan, not me. And for Black women, the vitriol and violence can be not only unbearable, but deadly. For us, "safe spaces" aren't just about feeling good and having fun, but creating an environment in which we are safely able to flourish, thrive, and grow. ·

Black-women-led spaces work hard to consider my lived experiences as well as my varied intersections, in order to offer me an opportunity to be part of a community that not only allows me to come as I am, but actively works in non-Black spaces to make sure that I continue to feel valued. Black Girls Skate, Black Girls Swim, and Black Girls Surf are all fan spaces that give a voice to those who have otherwise been voiceless in these sports. This is why Black-women-led fan spaces in predominantly white-led sports institutions remain powerful, precious, and unable to be authentically replicated. And really, they shouldn't be. The unique intersections of these movements create the circumstances for small organizations to develop into sacred spaces that produce a particularly enriching activism, with social change benefits that affect a variety of marginalizations. When we succeed, we uplift those around us; that's how it works because this is part of our shared value system, rooted deeply in our ancestors and in community.

I see it when I meet other Black women working in hockey, who identify a gap and proceed to do what they can to fill it, because they love the game and want to make it better for those around them. If there is a secret recipe to Black Girl Magic, it is in this intentionality of community care, in how we uplift our sisters, daughters, nieces, and friends; in how we naturally lead, build, and thrive when given the proper tools for success, and how we pass those tools down and around our own community spaces in order to build up and out. These magical qualities are less mystical and more action-based, and guided by empathy, openness, and thoughtful discernment. We possess these qualities because we understand that there is a purpose greater than our individual experiences, and we have the power within ourselves to facilitate positive change.

I'm not saying it's easy, or that it doesn't sometimes feel unfair to have what feels like a heavy cultural responsibility in every space I enter, simply because if I don't acknowledge the gaps and help fill them in then no one will. But I will say that I love Black women, and we deserve to be the main characters every once in a while. We deserve to have spaces that centre our needs, our experiences, and our skills. That uplift us and remind us of our value. This is not exclusionary, because when Black women lead, all intersectional identities benefit from our communal vision for a better society that offers equity to the most marginalized. For some, being asked to develop empathy, to consider pronouns and gender identity, to acknowledge class disparity and privilege, to recognize systemic racism in the institutions, families, and lives that they lead feels like oppression. This is not my problem, however, and nor is it my focus—which of course is the issue for my Twitter comment trolls. I am Black all year long, and that's important, because my experiences and my intersections give me power, give me strength, and give me the ability to speak to a variety of issues that matter. *It's Black Girl Magic, baby.*

A Good Day for Hockey

That morning, she makes sure to bring only what she can carry onto the train and into the Staples Center. She won't be home until after midnight. She decides to skip out on work early in order to take two trains through two counties. She runs over the schedule in her head. *From campus, to the local train station, a transfer midway, then she must catch an Uber at Union Station to get to Staples Center right in time for end-of-the-day, middle-of-the-week Downtown L.A. traffic. The Oilers vs. Kings game starts at seven.* Timeliness is important to her.

Underneath the steady thrum of anxiety she always feels while travelling alone sits an anticipation of the evening ahead. Three hours from now and sixty miles away, she will meet Marge and Barbara underneath the Gretzky statue in front of the Staples Center. Marge is bringing two handmade signs and has begrudgingly decided to share. They plan to head down to the glass, cheer for Looch and only Looch, and try to get on the official Oilers Twitter account.

When she finally slips into her window seat and pulls on her Oilers beanie, the tension in her neck begins to loosen. Now it's up to the travel gods. *Nothing more to do.*

She tucks a pair of headphones into her ears and turns to gaze out the window. The rhythm of the train, the push and pull underfoot, mesmerizes her. She puts on the *Trouble Man* soundtrack and leans back to watch the cities fly by.

Ten minutes into the second train ride, they get stuck in Whittier. Most of the time, she works travel mishaps into the planning, but it's hard to know what to anticipate with public transportation. There is someone on the tracks, or some*thing*, and it takes almost half an hour for them to get back on their way. At Union Station, she's got to find a bathroom, of course, and then it's into an Uber for the two miles between Alameda and Figueroa, which takes twenty-seven minutes. The driver keeps asking her questions, even though she's got her headphones in. She prefers silent drivers; the ones who let her sit in the back and pretend to be busy working on her phone. Today, the driver is asking her questions about hockey, the teams, and her affiliation. It's tiring but she's a recovering people-pleaser, so she gives half-assed answers until he finally gives up. They crawl through traffic, creeping closer to their destination, slower than she would like. When the arena is in sight, she hops out, takes a last look in the back seat, and thanks him. Traffic clogs the streets, but she knows that the Gretzky statue stands just around the corner. When the statue comes into sight, she grumbles the usual prayer under her breath.

Mario Lemieux is better. They're both problematic white men, anyway. Go Pens.

Marge and Barbara meet her exactly when and where they said they would. She loves her timely friends. At the gate, security forces Barbara to either throw her Oilers sign away or tear it in half because it's too big, which seems incredibly arbitrary. Barbara rips the sign in half, because she worked on it for hours at Marge's house that afternoon. When they finally appease security and enter the arena, they head directly to the team store to ask for tape. The Kings' arena staff doesn't seem too keen on helping a road fan put their sign back together, but after a few tries, Barbara reassembles it and they head down to the glass for warmies.

When they get to the ice, the last of the travel anxiety falls away and is replaced with a very specific hockey-based anxiety. She's got a variety of anxieties, actually. To be fair, it's always weird walking into a hockey arena. She becomes fully aware of her melanin, and watches other hockey fans eyeball her the entire night—wondering, probably, if she's lost or famous. She tries to ignore them and focus on the game, and it works, most of the time. She decidedly does not think about the last time she attended a hockey game at Staples Center with Marge. The time when some forty-year-old white dude came up to her and tried to get her to take a picture with his friend because, as the dude put it, his friend "liked Black girls." Like she was some sort of novelty or something. For hockey, maybe, but what the actual fuck? And when she said no, he put his hands on her and screamed, "Don't be a bitch! It's just a picture!" before Marge told him to fuck off with her entire tiny being. When his friend stepped in to stop the interaction, he simply excused the bad behaviour and then turned to tell his buddy, "They're probably dykes anyway," before walking down the hall and disappearing into the crowd. The worst part was that these guys were sitting in her and Marge's section the entire game, and so all she could do was stare at the guy's buffalo-plaid shirt as the two men sat in the stands, only a few feet away, enjoying themselves thoroughly after harassing her in the halls.

No, she is not thinking about that today.

Instead, she is focused on making sure Looch notices Marge's signs at the glass and making sure to piss off as many Kings fans as possible with her ridiculous goal cellies. *Sorry not sorry.* When they get to their seats in the lower bowl, it's an Edmonton-heavy section, and then the focus is on the game and bonding with other road fans in the stands. Every time the Oilers score, they all jump up in unison, celebrating the hard-fought goal. They don't win that night, but it doesn't matter. They still have a blast.

After the game, Marge drives her all the way home, through two counties, across multiple highways, and they laugh together the entire way. Barbara is only in town from Minnesota for a few more days. She and Marge have plans to go to another Kings game before she leaves, and this time cheer for the home team. Marge drops her off close to midnight, and then turns around and drives all the way back to L.A.

As she heads into the dark and still house, she sends Marge a few bucks for gas. After a quick shower, she sits in bed looking through pictures and videos from the night, posting the best ones to her Instagram and Twitter accounts. As the adrenaline from the night slowly drains from her body, it is all she can do to keep her eyes open. Finally, she sets down her phone, closes her eyes to the darkness of the room, and lets out a contented sigh. It was a good day for hockey. It was a very good day.

THE WHITE PEOPLE CHAPTER

Reasons why this chapter is going to be hard to write:

1. The white people I genuinely love might get their feelings hurt. Liberal white folks notoriously find it difficult to identify and acknowledge their part in systemic racism, particularly those with Black or biracial family members and close friends.

2. White people feelings. Goodness! I've noticed they really don't want to feel the discomfort that comes with understanding the effects of racism or misogynoir.

3. White fragility. I think that's the main reason that this chapter is going to be difficult.

4. Figuring out my target audience for this chapter, too, is a thing. This whole book has been for Black women. So who am I writing this chapter for? White folks, or Black folks on how to deal with white folks in hockey?

5. . . .

Teaching white folks how to be better to Black folks is honestly so triggering for me. Reiterating my humanity, or making people "see me" as a human being "just like them" is actually super bigoted and not fun for marginalized folks at all. Plus, who am I writing this chapter for? White people who support anti-racism work in hockey? White people who don't? When every other story in this book has been centred on and curated for Black women, why change it up now? To appease white supremacy?

As I sit down to pen what I've lovingly been calling "The White People Chapter," what I want to make clear is that this entire book—each essay, interview, joke, and blessing—is meant for Black women. "The White People Chapter" is also for us. What I want to do is lay out some ways that white folks have helped advance anti-racism in hockey, and the ways that they have hindered it. I want to share conversations I've had with white women who work quietly (and sometimes loudly, when they need to) in the spaces they occupy to subvert racism and uplift Black women. I want to also shine a light on the toxicity of white feminism and how white women uphold systemic racism because ultimately they benefit from it. But first I want to say something directly to White People.

Dear White People,

Do better.

Sincerely,

Renee

First of all, let me begin by saying: some of my closest friends are white! My mama is white. There are white folks getting paid right now to work for my non-profit focusing on Black women in hockey, Black Girl Hockey Club. I grew up surrounded by white people, going to church and to school at predominantly white institutions (PWIs), with many white bosses, besties, and interests throughout my life. I am very familiar with the inner workings of white folks; I have lived among them since the day I was born. When I tell folks this, they are often confused about how I (and if I really have) divested from whiteness. How can I be biracial and divest from whiteness? How can I love my white mama and friends and divest from whiteness? How can I work at a PWI and divest from whiteness? What the heck does "divest from whiteness" even mean? Well, to begin with, we have to define and identify the term *whiteness*.

The concept of whiteness began to develop during the European Enlightenment, as a means of dehumanization and differentiation that continued during chattel slavery and beyond. Much like gender and sexuality, race is a social construct created for the purpose of control by the ruling class. I don't mean simply *nationality* or *ethnicity*, which denotes an individual's country of origin. According to the Smithsonian National Museum of African American History and Culture, races are defined as *groupings*, "into which humankind is considered (in various theories or contexts) to be divided on the basis of physical characteristics or shared ancestry." So, society—with our various theories and contexts—defines racial groups by aesthetics in addition to ancestral qualities. Meaning, individuals can have an ancestry that may or may not align with the aesthetic qualities that society deems "white." A Black person can "act" white, so to speak, but not *be* white, because whiteness separates itself from the rest of humanity using aesthetic *and* ancestral qualities as signifiers. Meaning, race is arbitrary! For example, during Black History Month in 2023, there was a TikTok going around with the story of Lucy and Maria Aylmer, UK-born biological twins with the same Black mother and white father, although most people wouldn't believe it based on their appearance. The sisters are now in their teens: Lucy has pale white skin and red hair while Maria has a darker complexion and thick curly black hair. One sister has the physical characteristics (skin, hair texture, facial features) of a person of African descent. The other sister, who has a similar facial structure as her twin, also has very light skin, freckles, and auburn hair with a straight texture. Regardless of their identical ethnic makeup, aesthetically one twin might be considered white and the other one Black.

Because of colonization and chattel slavery, whiteness must mean more than just skin colour; it also includes a set of societal concepts based on the superiority of white people, customs, and culture. When white enslavers raped Black enslaved women over generations and their light-skinned babies had even lighter-skinned babies, the "one-drop rule" created a legal and government-sanctioned way to differentiate position and power using colourism. Through a series of laws based on physical and social markers, American society has spent the past 400 years defining whiteness on a sliding scale.

White supremacy also sees to it that class solidarity is steeped in racism and nearly impossible to achieve. Regardless of how poor a white person is, they are still at least white, and remain invested in the privileges of a white identity marker. In the United States, where chattel slavery created and sustained our earliest economies, the goalposts of whiteness continue to move. The one-drop rule remains a concept imbued in American culture, and while Lucy might be considered white in England, in the good ole U.S. of A, Lucy has a Black mama, therefore according to the American construct of race, Lucy is Black. She might be "passing," but that doesn't change the fact that the one-drop rule is a prevalent part of American societal standards, practices, and written and unwritten law. For too long, much of society has centred whiteness and made it out to be the dominant culture, when in fact Black and brown folks, Indigenous people, and immigrants continue to be the *global majority*—a term coined in 2003 by Black scholar Rosemary Campbell-Stevens and an intentional use of language disrupting the status quo. Our culture, our art, our politics, and our communities have value, even though we are told at every juncture that they do not, mostly so that capitalists upholding white supremacy can exploit and make money off of us. *Ahhh, yes, capitalism. Here we go,* folks who know me will say.

It's imperative to understand that racism is not only ugly and hateful, but profitable. Even worse, though, after the summer of 2020, anti-racism became a profitable industry for some—until, of course, it wasn't. While corporations rushed to create Diversity, Equity, and Inclusion roles, employment resource groups, and Inclusion and Belonging initiatives, according to a 2023 NBC article by Curtis Bunn, Black employees still only represent 3.8 per cent of chief diversity officers overall, with white people making up 76.1 per cent of the roles. Those of Hispanic or Latino origin make up 7.8 per cent and those of Asian origin make up 7.7 per cent.

Some may bring back my own words to argue: *But Renee! You said that white folks should use Google and do their own research and teach themselves how to not be racist!* But I also say that companies should PAY BLACK WOMEN when and if they are asked to do this work, so this is not the "gotcha!" moment you think it is. Even as the government, universities, and even the NHL roll back diversity initiatives, Black women are asked to fill in the gaps, often for free. Diversity, Equity, and Inclusion (or DEI) is a genre of motivational self-help that has taken over the corporate world as a Band-Aid for racism. Surface level DEI efforts are geared more toward easing white guilt than creating institutional change. Often times when Black women are brought into a company to help solve diversity issues, we are given little organizational support, sometimes outright pushback, and yet we are expected to solve the problems of racism within our industries. For primarily white-led institutions, it's a lot easier to focus on what makes white people feel better than to examine all the ways they've plundered and pillaged their way through civilized society. Organizations such as the highly rated firm White Men as Full Diversity Partners let their clients know right there in the name how important white men are in the fight for equality in the workplace. Centring white men, the most left-out of the intersections when we talk about diversity, reminds everyone how important white men are to every aspect of everything, even efforts to dismantle white supremacy. Thank goodness! I had almost forgotten! The importance!! Of White Men!!!

Heavy sigh . . . maybe I am talking a little bit to the white people here, sis, my bad. This is obviously day-one shit.

So why centre whiteness, white feelings, white flight, or white rights during discussions about racism?

You know why.

Still talking to white people here, sis, bear with me.

It's because racism lines folks' pockets, and keeping marginalized communities at the margins *(ahem)* is a profitable industry that fuels global capitalism because the point of capitalism is to separate the haves from the have-nots, which reinforces white supremacy and vice versa. So when I say over mimosas at brunch to my friends, and basically anyone who will listen, that capitalism is the root of all evil, I mean capitalism is built upon and sustains white supremacy. They go hand in hand.

To combat the insidious nature of racism, which will always try to find a way to take root in our communities, our organizations, and our institutions, we must decolonize those institutions and divest from these systems. In terms of hockey, we must free the sport from the societal and cultural effects of colonization and support the restitution and revitalization of Black and Indigenous Peoples in these spaces. Now, that may sound extremely difficult and out of one individual's grasp—and, dear reader, you would be correct. But never fear! There are individual actions that we can all take in the spaces that we occupy in order to make them more equitable for all marginalized folks. There are co-conspirators inside corporations who work daily to shift the status quo and make their schools, workplaces, and homes safe spaces for Black, brown, disabled, and LGBTQ folks. Not only that, but there are white people who actively listen to, learn from, and support leaders who represent a variety of intersections, not because these acts will benefit them as white people, but because they are human beings sharing the planet with other human beings.

Ah, but a moral argument never shifted a racist's perspective, and that's not the point of this book. The point is to share stories that you haven't heard before. Stories about Black women in hockey. In this chapter, though, I want to share a couple of conversations between me and my white girlfriends, who support and ride hard for Black Girl Hockey Club and other organizations that focus on marginalized identities that, frankly, they do not occupy.

Usually, the first question on my mind when I see white folks in spaces that are meant to centre Black women is: *Why are you here?* I want to know what it is that they find valuable in this space, because *I* know what is so special about Black Girl Hockey Club, and I need them to say it out loud and acknowledge what *they* stand to gain by being in *our* community. Then I need to know (if you are reading this and you are a non-Black woman who works closely with me and BGHC, you already recognize this line of questioning) what will they offer to our community in exchange for what they will gain. Will they listen? Decentre themselves? Will they stand up for me when I'm not in the room? When there's no one who looks like me in the room? Step aside to make space for Black women and other marginalized communities? Will they do their own research? Find their own answers and leave me out of the guilt, anger, and confusion that white people feel when they begin to understand and acknowledge their own part in upholding white supremacy and racism in their families, workplaces, and friend groups? Those feelings definitely should be examined, but not by me. Please! I and other Black folks should be left out of any inner revelations, or examinations of racist puns or sayings or actions or brands white folks have been using since forever and *just never realized they were bad*—unless we explicitly say that we have the capacity to take on your racial awakening.

This type of education is simply not my calling, as you can probably tell. Schooling white people on how to treat me and members of other marginalized communities with respect and care is not how I like to expend my energy. I'd much rather focus on how to uplift Black women, and how to create community spaces that continue to move forward, instead of backtracking by focusing energy on placating white people when they feel bad about benefiting from white supremacy. I am particularly wary of white feminism, which historically has had no problem co-opting movements from Black women and then throwing us under the proverbial bus when times get hard (*Susan B. Anthony, I'm looking at you bitch*). I'm big on giving folks their flowers, but I cannot give flowers to folks for simply treating humans like humans. It's giving pick-me vibes.

You are probably as curious as I am about how long it takes for white folks to start using their status as "white" against us in our own spaces, and the ways that BGHC combats centring whiteness on a regular basis. So let's get into it.

I often say that "you don't have to be Black and you don't have to be a woman to be part of the Black Girl Hockey Club." It's a cutesy line I tell mostly men or white folks when we talk about the values of BGHC. It makes them feel comfortable, which, my bad, I know isn't really my thing, but technically it's true. What I don't get into on larger stages is the fact that this particular invitation is conditional. In order to *maintain* access to BGHC spaces, people who are not Black women must buy into the idea that they are not more important or special than anyone else, particularly Black women, in BGHC. We are the main characters here, honey! Their tears, their fears, and their biases are not inherently put first in BGHC, and they must take "no" as a complete answer. Each time BGHC gains a new potential volunteer who will have access to sensitive information about our core audience, I sit down with them face to face via Zoom, and we have a short chat. I ask hard questions and expect thoughtful responses. I won't say that there are no wrong answers, because of course there are. I must be able to trust each person who comes into this space with my peace and the peace of every Black woman who allows us to help make her hockey experience a good one, and I will err on the side of caution every damn time. Regardless of race or gender, if the vibes are off, I have learned to listen to my instincts and to stand up for this space I lead. I also am not afraid to admit when I'm wrong. I'm fallible and don't know everything, but I know what makes me and my friends uncomfortable and icky, so I start there and then learn to adapt. I also listen to those who occupy similar spaces as me, folks I trust as colleagues, friends, and peers. I reach out, I ask for help, and I confer with other BIPOC women and LGBTQ folk, because marginalized communities are not a monolith. My biases and privilege affect the way I see and engage with the world, and so do yours.

In a sit-down interview for this chapter, one of my first-ever hockey friends, Christy Brown, a white girl hockey fan living in Minnesota, explains in simple terms how white folks can effectively engage in helping make hockey more equitable for all.

"You've got to do the work. Not everybody is going to be like me and do their homework necessarily. But Google is your freaking friend. Stop relying on people of colour for labour, especially if it's emotionally intensive labour of any sort. You have to do the work, you have to educate yourself, and you have to do the work on yourself. The issues around equity and inclusion in sports are not a theoretical thing. They are a real thing that has been perpetuated over years and years and years and years, and that's not going to get undone, and it's not going to get better overnight. It's going to take white people being accountable and willing to be called out. I'm not even going to do the whole 'called in'! Sometimes people need to be put in their place. And that can be done with good intentions and love, or it can be kind of a swat on the nose, and being like, *No, stop it!*"

I met Christy on the #GoStars hashtag on Twitter back in 2015. Her Twitter profile seemed on the up and up; she worked in higher ed, like me, was a fan of the Stars and Pens, also like me, and seemed to be open to different intersections. Her friend list is varied and she has never had a problem being vocal about the causes she cares about, either on or off social media. As we speak frankly about the hockey landscape, I want to understand how and if Christy's engagement in a sport she has loved since she was a child has changed over time, particularly in recent years. I'm also curious to hear her take on whether or not hockey is actually a fixable institution. Her insightful answers call into question current efforts in professional sports and the need for a top-down culture change.

"My priorities have shifted and my involvement in hockey has looked very different because of COVID. A lot of what I wanted to do or what I would have done, pre-pandemic, particularly living in Minnesota with George Floyd last summer, was very, very different. I'm very much on the 'defund police' train now, whereas previously I was like, oh, maybe you know, we can reform. Whatever. No. Burn it to the ground, because it's all fruit from a poisoned tree. Part of me wonders if hockey needs to do that as well, you know, thinking about what culture change actually looks like. There's a lot of people in my own life that I've had conversations with that have said, *Oh, well, we can't do this, because of that.* Well, just because it's always been done in a particular way doesn't mean it always has to be that way. And you know, history is obdurate. It's resistant to change. Moments of change are seen as sort of this big 'kaboom' moment, and not the product of a lot of behind the scenes work. Thinking about the Civil Rights movement in the '60s, it wasn't just the March on Washington, it was years and years and years of work that led to the Civil Rights Act. And you know, again, cultural change still hasn't happened. And so I think hockey is very much the same way."

Christy is getting heated now and doesn't hold back the annoyance on her face or with her body language. "I think white fragility is absolutely a real thing. You need to interrogate that fragility. When you find yourself kind of getting your hackles raised, or when you are called out, or when you're told 'nope,' this isn't your conversation, this isn't your space. Just, you know, the people who are like, *Well, it doesn't sound so inclusive if it's just for Black girls.* Like that was me responding to a whole bunch of people yesterday on Twitter, and, I know, don't feed the trolls because whatever, but sometimes just . . ." She trails off, frustrated.

"It's the wilful ignorance for me. Hockey culture can be very much consuming, from what I understand, having never played, especially in Canada. You certainly hear about that idea of hockey culture. But *everybody's* human and everybody consumes media, unless maybe you're a Mennonite like what's his face? James Reimer; he grew up as a Mennonite. But you cannot—" She interrupts herself, backtracking. "No, you can. You *can* ignore issues, you can ignore problems. But don't try to feed me a line of crap that *Oh, I didn't know it was an issue.* No. You know, I think it goes back to the golden rule: 'Do unto others as you would have them do unto you.' Or what about the platinum rule? Do unto others as they would have them? Have you done unto them? You know? That seems so basic."

Later, we say our goodbyes with promises to catch up again soon, to talk hockey and try to forget some of the drama of the outside world. The world doesn't make that easy, though, with COVID and travel restrictions, life changes, and all the other stuff that comes up. We finally do connect again, again for this book. Christy is a language phenom (she speaks five—Russian, German, English, French, and a wee bit of Spanish), a grammar nerd (as am I), and the first person I thought of when I realized I needed help transcribing some interviews. She offered to help, and when she extends that type of offer—when any of my non-Black allies do—instead of brushing it off and explaining it away as a nicety, I listen and try to find a way to accept help.

So Christy helped me sift through a couple dozen hour-plus-long interviews and painstakingly transcribed each one.

She was a godsend! Of course I paid her—because we compensate women around here—at her very discounted rate, and she continues to come through when I need her. That is what an ally does, and how we can start to balance the scales of power and privilege, one equitable act at a time.

I've known Christy Brown for almost a decade. She taught me a lot about the game of hockey and the immobility of the culture around the sport. But moving into these high-level hockey spaces and finding allies way up at the top of the sport feels like a whole different ball game, so to speak. At the highest levels of hockey there are very few women in leadership positions and positions of power, and most are white women. Kim Davis, at the NHL; Delvina Morrow and Tracey McCants Lewis at the Pittsburgh Penguins; Stephanie Jackson at USA Hockey: these are exceptional women, and the exception to the very white, very male spaces they occupy. More likely, when I hop on a Zoom call or attend an event around topics of inclusion in hockey, I will be surrounded by white folks who are there to listen and learn.

It is in these spaces that I feel most in need of an organization like BGHC and the programming we do, particularly the Get Uncomfortable Campaign. The GUC is the only BGHC program that engages directly with non-Black people in a way that promotes education, intentionality, and awareness. When we started the program, it was really a way for us to push individuals and organizations to state plainly their intentions around Black issues. We start by asking folks to "Get Uncomfortable" and discuss issues from hiring practices to police brutality, and then we parse out who is serious and who just wants an audience to *think* they're serious. When teams or businesses decide they want to sign the GUC Pledge, we make sure that they know the commitment doesn't just end with their name; we consider signing the pledge a privilege, not a right, and it means something to us over at Black Girl Hockey Club. If your name is on our signatory list, we hold you accountable when we must, call you in when we can, and offer our knowledge and experience to help grow a more equitable space for marginalized folks in hockey. We do this not as a way to centre white folks, but to address their place in advocacy work that lifts up Black women.

So many white people say they want to help but have no idea what that means. The GUC gives Black Girl Hockey Club a way to identify and connect with potential co-conspirators on our own terms. It is clear that BGHC does not need white people to accomplish our goals as a community space for Black women. We have a Black-led board of directors, and a high number of Black volunteers, contract workers, and donors helping us move forward in our mission. But I'm not a segregationist! I believe that valuing multiculturalism helps me be a better educator, parent, and citizen of the world. I enjoy learning from and engaging with different people, and prefer to work with individuals and organizations who hold similar values. But white supremacy and capitalism really do have folks in a chokehold! Apparently there are many good excuses for why equity cannot happen *right now*; so many valid and long-winded explanations as to why marginalized folks should wait, be happy, expect less, be satisfied with what we have, and stop asking for more. They can't just fire the old white men who occupy the top positions in these spaces! They've got to leave or die, so no one feels bad! Of course, if their sons or friends or proteges want to enter the space, they will make room, but for marginalized folks, the timing just can't seem to ever be right.

This half-assed commitment to inclusion creates room for White Men as Full Diversity Partners and leaves out Black Professionals Able to Pivot Their Talent, LGBTQ Folks Committed to Community Growth, and Disabled People Ready to Lend Their Expertise. What is the purpose of Diversity and Inclusion efforts in organizations that continue to cater to white fragility?

Optics.

So how do we combat that?

Tara Slone, former co-host of the Canadian feel-good television show *Rogers Hometown Hockey*, has a few ideas on the subject. In February 2021, she invited me to be a guest on the Sportsnet series *Top of Her Game*. The piece can be found on YouTube, and it was the first time Tara and I worked together. Later that same year, I invited Tara to join a panel of allies for the BGHC Juneteenth conversation about race and hockey, to discuss with our group the ways in which she had succeeded and failed at allyship. Over the years, I have watched Tara use her proximity to power in hockey spaces to challenge the hegemony of the sport from the inside out, and her willingness to amplify the work of BIPOC women in sports makes Tara a great co-conspirator in spaces that marginalized folks don't often occupy.

When we talked about this book in May 2022, it was a month before Sportsnet cancelled *Hometown Hockey* and effectively let Tara go from the network.

"I think like a lot of other people, I am the squeaky wheel," Tara began. "But the squeaky wheel is not always rewarded, you know? I've been punished. I've definitely been punished, sort of tacitly or otherwise, for speaking my mind. I know that I'm not the most popular person at my network. I know that there are a lot of mutterings and murmurings and people who wish I would be quiet. But I have also learned that that has to be okay. You know, there's just no other way to do it, and it's unfair. But I think that's how I do it. If you see me on social media, I tend to kind of come back with fire when people are trolling me, and that's my style. That's not everybody's style! That's just kind of who I am.

"Sometimes it's so insidious, you know? Often it's *so* insidious. Like the conversations you have where people look past you, and I will say this, and it's fine to be open about it. I mean, I work with Ron MacLean, who is, you know, one of the most lauded hockey broadcasters in this country, and obviously has been in the business for a long time. There are a fair number of interviews that we'll do with NHL alumni where they literally don't even look at me."

In November 2022, Tara accepted a position with the San Jose Sharks in Southern California and committed herself to continuing on a path of intentionality in her personal and professional lives. As soon as I heard that Tara planned to work here in the fine state of California, I reached out to let her know that BGHC had an event in the works with the Sharks during February 2023, to celebrate Black History Month. I hoped the two of us might finally meet in person, but it ended up that neither of us happened to be in San Jose the weekend of the Black Girl Hockey Club meet-up. Instead, we scheduled a chat on Zoom for Tara's new Sharks podcast, *The Undercurrent*, and caught up on what we'd each been up to over the past few months.

For Tara, working in San Jose had been an incredibly positive experience. She was hosting her own podcast, doing broadcast and on-air stuff with the team, and had the time and the chance to do the work she loved on her own terms. It seemed to be the opportunity she hadn't known she was waiting for the last time we spoke.

"You know, when we did the Juneteenth event with BGHC [in 2021], the thing that Bryant McBride said to me that really stuck with me is I talked about walking the tightrope between, you know, being part of the broadcast—the NHL broadcaster in Canada is Sportsnet—and speaking my mind and using my voice. He said, 'It's time to get off the tightrope.' And I really, I feel like I'm off now. I feel like I'm off and it's kind of scary. Maybe I'm hanging on by my fingertips, but I don't think I'm treading the line so much anymore. I recognize that I have a certain position and privilege to be able to use my voice. So that's all I can do."

Recently, the word *ally* has come to be seen as more performative than helpful. On June 2, 2020, a social media trend called #BlackoutTuesday had more than 28 million users posting black squares to their Instagram accounts in solidarity with the Black Lives Matter movement and the protests taking place at the time. Led by the efforts of two Black women, what started as an attempt to urge the music industry to show care and support toward Black Lives Matter activists using the hashtag #TheShowMustBePaused was quickly co-opted by people on social media who wanted to join in on the trend. Unfortunately, well-meaning "allies" unintentionally used and subsequently clogged up the actual #BlackLivesMatter hashtag meant to connect Black organizers all across the globe. The criticism from Black activists was scathing—the black squares, the co-opting of the hashtag, the trend-hopping without any context—it all highlighted the performative nature of this type of allyship. For non-BIPOC folks who wish to authentically engage in anti-racism, whether personally or professionally, the two most important things to understand are a) the power of your voice, and b) the necessity of your silence. In spaces where whiteness offers power and privilege, our white-identifying co-conspirators should use their whiteness to support those who are not uplifted by systems of oppression. In this same vein, allies invited into spaces meant for marginalized folks must also recognize the power of their silence and use the opportunity to learn from the experiences of others. This is the only way that I can see to decentre whiteness and decolonize our institutions that doesn't involve burning it all to the ground, as per Christy's suggestion. But what does this look like in hockey?

Well, for me, I tend to come back to my favourite team to watch and to work with, the Pittsburgh Penguins. At this point, you should have seen it coming! In 2019, the Penguins went outside of their hockey bubble and hired both Tracey McCants Lewis and Delvina Morrow, two Black women working in very different departments who, in this hegemonic space, became fast friends and allies to one another. Not only that, they both immediately began working with BGHC to help develop a stronger relationship with local Black hockey fans and players. But I've waxed eloquent about the Black Girl Magic of Tracey and Delvina in previous chapters; you can find their stories there. What I want to focus on is what my favourite PWI, the Pittsburgh Penguins, did right.

The Penguins structurally and financially supported the endeavours of these Black women to engage with "non-traditional" local and travelling audiences, and I've been lucky enough to clock how the relationship that Black folks in Pittsburgh have with Penguins hockey has changed. In 2021, the Pittsburgh Penguins Foundation hired Jaden Lindo, a young Black native of Brampton, Ontario (and a 2014 Penguins draftee), to be the manager of its Community Hockey Programs. In this role, Jaden works with the Pittsburgh I.C.E. (Inclusion Creates Equality) program and engages directly with Black players and fans.

As the relationships in Pittsburgh between the Penguins, BGHC, and local Black communities began to strengthen, the concept for the Willie O'Ree Academy was born. In the fall of 2022, the academy opened its doors for the first time at the Hunt Armory, a facility that the Penguins had worked for over a year to gain access to in order to host community programming for Black youth. The purpose of the WOR Academy is to give local Black kids who already play hockey an opportunity to work on enriching their skill set in an environment that has been built to help them thrive and create community—plus, it's all free.

The Hunt Armory is not directly in the downtown core of Pittsburgh, a mistake I, a non-local, have made in print before and must clarify. The rink is above the Hill District, a predominantly Black area in the East End neighbourhood of Shadyside, which boasts an eclectic arts and social scene. But the twenty-minute bus ride to Shadyside is a lot more accessible to kids living in the urban areas than the UPMC Lemieux Sports Complex, the Penguins' practice rink in the township of Cranberry, an hour outside of downtown. What had started as engaging in inclusive hiring practices turned into an opportunity for the team to meet the needs of local Black hockey players and fans in a unique and exciting way.

Contrary to popular belief, Geno isn't the only reason I love the Pens. From the diverse staff to the unwavering support of allies within the organization, I root for the Pittsburgh Penguins because of the ethos of the team as a whole. The narrative of the Pens is this—they were losers for a long time, but had some amazing coaches and players that brought magic to the game of hockey in Pittsburgh, and developed a loyal fanbase in the city. At some point, someone tried to sell the team to Kansas City?? And then Mario Lemieux put in his own cash and bought the team in 1999 so that it wouldn't have to leave Pittsburgh. He got cancer and stopped playing, but came back to play a season with Sidney Crosby. When the Pens drafted Crosby in 2005 and then Malkin arrived in 2006 (yes, they won the lottery twice!) the team was *really* bad. They added some more core players to the roster—Marc-André Fleury and Kris Letang—and made it to the Stanley Cup Final in 2008, only to lose in six to the Detroit Red Wings. Then they made it back to the final in 2009, against Detroit again, and this time they won the Cup! This was all before my time as a fan, but I've read the stories and watched the documentaries, and talked to enough fans to know how important this team is to their city.

The wonderful thing is, the organization legitimately seems to care about the local community. They continue to grow in meaningful ways that help maintain a love of hockey among the citizens of the diverse city of Pittsburgh. In 2021 they hired Brian Burke to be President of Hockey Operations, and Burkie brings a fierce allyship with the LGBTQ community in addition to a willingness to listen to all marginalized communities and use his influence to shift power dynamics. While he moved on in 2023 to the PWHLPA, we both sit on the board of the Carnegie Initiative, and I have observed him listening and learning from marginalized communities and then taking that knowledge into his work to make hockey spaces more equitable for all. This is the measure of a proper ally, and it gives me hope for the future of this sport. To know that men like Burkie—a "traditional" hockey executive, former player, and middle-aged, cisgender, able-bodied straight white man—and *I* can conspire together to make hockey a better place for anyone who has ever felt abandoned in the margins of hockey—well, that's exciting stuff! Burkie, Christy, Tara, and the countless other co-conspirators I've met in hockey spaces remind me that intersectional markers do not denote my enemies, and nor should they for you, dear reader. You don't have to be Black and you don't have to be a girl to be part of Black Girl Hockey Club, you just have to support our mission. It's as simple and as complicated as that.

ACKNOWLEDGEMENTS

I wish to acknowledge with gratitude all the Black women, activists, and co-conspirators who sat and talked hockey with me over the course of writing and researching this book. Thank you for letting me tell this story.

I also want to say thank you to those who helped bring this book to life with their insights, in particular Joe, for needing to see this book published as much as I did; Rebecca, for gifting me with easy deadlines and for her steady eye; Brenna and Evan, my tag team agents, cheerleaders, and think tank; Liz, for introducing me to hockey gently and letting me love the Pens; Christy B, for researching, brainstorming, and organizing when I needed you; Isabel, the real brains of the operation; Lola, Christy, Mom, Pop, Windsor, Mama Cathy, Sam, Jazz, Merville, Melissa, the *other* Melissa, Dr. J, and Shireen, my support system; my trusted first reader and dear sister, Sarah; BGHC, my guiding light; and all the group chats that witnessed me rant, cry, and birth this book into existence with rapt attention and unwavering belief.

WORKS CITED

Author's note: the interviews throughout this book have been edited for length and clarity.

Beck, Koa. *White Feminism: From the Suffragettes to Influencers and Who They Leave Behind*. New York: Atria Books, 2021.

Bergan, Brooke. "Argument 1." In *Storyville: A Hidden Mirror*. Wakefield, RI, and London: Asphodel Press, 1994.

Cargle, Rachel. "When Feminism Is White Supremacy in Heels." *Harper's Bazaar*, August 16, 2018. https://www.harpersbazaar.com/culture/politics/a22717725/what-is-toxic-white-feminism/.

"Chief Diversity Officer Demographics and Statistics in the US." Zippia. Last modified April 5, 2024. https://www.zippia.com/chief-diversity-officer-jobs/demographics/.

Conrad, Earl. *Jim Crow America*. New York: Duell, Sloan and Pearce, 1947.

Crenshaw, Kimberlé. "Demarginalizing the Intersection of Race and Sex: A Black Feminist Critique of Antidiscrimination Doctrine, Feminist Theory and Antiracist Politics." *University of Chicago Legal Forum*, vol. 1, article 8 (1989): 139–67. http://chicagounbound.uchicago.edu/uclf/vol1989/iss1/8.

Denton-Hurst, Tembe. "It Doesn't Matter If We Behave." The Cut, April 10, 2023. https://www.thecut.com/2023/04/black-women-professionalism-workplace-homebodies-book-essay.html.

Du Bois, W.E.B. "The Talented Tenth." In *The Negro Problem: A Series of Articles by Representative American Negroes of To-day*, edited by Booker T. Washington, 31–75. New York: James Pott & Company, 1903.

Hockey Diversity Alliance (@TheOfficialHDA). "HDA releases this statement on behalf of Trevor Daley regarding the Soo Greyhounds removal of the banner and number of John Vanbiesbrouck from the rafters of GFL Memorial Gardens." *Twitter*, January 30, 2024. https://x.com/TheOfficialHDA/status/1752406816301129914?s=20.

Jones, Nicholas, Rachel Marks, Roberto Ramirez, and Merarys Ríos-Vargas. "2020 Census Illuminates Racial and Ethnic Composition of the Country." August 12, 2021. https://www.census.gov/library/stories/2021/08/improved-race-ethnicity-measures-reveal-united-states-population-much-more-multiracial.html.

Kaplan, Emily. "Women's hockey players' association adds Sarah Nurse to board to fix 'blind spot.'" ESPN, September 2, 2020. https://www.espn.com/nhl/story/_/id/29794679/women-hockey-players-association-adds-sarah-nurse-board-fix-blind-spot.

Lorde, Audre. "Poetry Is Not a Luxury." In *Sister Outsider*, 24-27. New York: Penguin Books, 2020.

Mills, Charles W. "White Ignorance." In *Race and Epistemologies of Ignorance*, edited by Shannon Sullivan and Nancy Tuana, 13–38. Albany: State University of New York Press, 2007.

Moon, Dreama G., and Michelle A. Holling. "'White supremacy in heels': (white) feminism, white supremacy, and discursive violence." *Communication and Critical/Cultural Studies*, vol. 17, no. 2 (June 2020): 253–60. https://doi.org/10.1080 /14791420.2020.1770819.

"Race and Racial Identity." National Museum of African American History and Culture. Accessed April 29, 2024. https://nmaahc.si.edu/learn/talking-about-race/topics/race-and -racial-identity#:~:text=The%20dictionary's%20definition%20 of%20race,ranked%20as%20superior%20and%20inferior.

Reuter, Edward Byron. *The Mulatto in the United States*. New York: Haskell House Publishers, 1969. First published 1918 by R.G. Badger.

Carnegie, Herbert H. The Future Aces Creed. Copyright 1962, 1988, 1997, 2007 by H.H. Carnegie and B.Y. Carnegie. https://futureaces.org/about-us/.

Tinker, Saroya (@saroyatinker71). "WE, as a league do not want support from ANY openly racist platform." *Twitter*, January 25, 2021. https://x.com/saroyatinker71/status/135391385985006387 4?s=20.